T. W. Rollestone

**The Teaching of Epictetus**

Being the Encheiridion of Epictetus. With selections from the Dissertations and Fragments.

T. W. Rollestone

**The Teaching of Epictetus**
*Being the Encheiridion of Epictetus. With selections from the Dissertations and Fragments.*

ISBN/EAN: 9783337175306

Printed in Europe, USA, Canada, Australia, Japan

Cover: Foto ©Paul-Georg Meister /pixelio.de

More available books at **www.hansebooks.com**

# CONTENTS.

|  |  | PAGE |
|---|---|---|
| INTRODUCTION | . . . . . . | ix |
| CLEANTHES' HYMN TO ZEUS | . . . . . | 1 |

## BOOK I.

| Chap. | I. The Beginning of Philosophy | . . . | 3 |
| Chap. | II. On the Natural Conceptions | . . . | 7 |
| Chap. | III. The Master-Faculty | . . . | 9 |
| Chap. | IV. The Nature of the Good | . . . | 12 |
| Chap. | V. The Promise of Philosophy | . . . | 14 |
| Chap. | VI. The Way of Philosophy | . . . | 15 |
| Chap. | VII. To the Learner | . . . | 20 |
| Chap. | VIII. The Cynic | . . . | 23 |

## BOOK II.

| Chap. | I. On Genuine and Borrowed Beliefs | . . | 40 |
| Chap. | II. The Game of Life | . . . | 45 |
| Chap. | III. Things are what they are | . . . | 50 |
| Chap. | IV. Three Steps to Perfection | . . | 52 |
| Chap. | V. That a man may be both bold and fearful | . | 54 |
| Chap. | VI. The Wise Man's Fear and the Fool's | . | 59 |
| Chap. | VII. Appearances False and True | . . | 60 |
| Chap. | VIII. How we should think as God's offspring | . | 63 |
| Chap. | IX. The Open Door | . . . | 70 |
| Chap. | X. Know Thyself | . . . | 73 |
| Chap. | XI. How we should bear ourselves towards evil men | . | 78 |
| Chap. | XII. The Voyage of Life | . . . | 80 |
| Chap. | XIII. The Mark of Effort | . . | 81 |
| Chap. | XIV. Faculties | . . . | 85 |
| Chap. | XV. Returns | . . . | 86 |
| Chap. | XVI. The Price of Tranquillity | . . | 86 |
| Chap. | XVII. A Choice | . . . | 87 |
| Chap. | XVIII. That where the Heart is the Bond is | . | 88 |
| Chap. | XIX. That we lament not from within | . | 89 |
| Chap. | XX. That a man may act his part but not choose it | . | 90 |
| Chap. | XXI. Distinctions | . . . | 92 |
| Chap. | XXII. That a man is sufficient to himself | . | 93 |
| Chap. | XXIII. That every man fulfil his own task | . | 94 |
| Chap. | XXIV. The World's Price for the World's Worth | . | 95 |
| Chap. | XXV. Aims of Nature | . . . | 97 |
| Chap. | XXVI. The Mind's Security | . . | 97 |
| Chap. | XXVII. That a Man should be One Man | . | 98 |

## CONTENTS.

### BOOK III.

| | | PAGE |
|---|---|---|
| Chap. I. | Obligations | 101 |
| Chap. II. | Against Epicurus | 102 |
| Chap. III. | Against the Epicureans and Academics | 104 |
| Chap. IV. | On Slavery | 109 |
| Chap. V. | To the Administrator of the Free Cities, who was an Epicurean | 110 |
| Chap. VI. | On Statecraft | 116 |
| Chap. VII. | On Friendship | 117 |
| Chap. VIII. | Time and Change | 123 |
| Chap. IX. | On Solitude | 133 |
| Chap. X. | Against the Contentious and Revengeful | 136 |

### BOOK IV.

| | | |
|---|---|---|
| Chap. I. | Of Religion | 141 |
| Chap. II. | Of Providence | 142 |
| Chap. III. | Of Providence | 146 |
| Chap. IV. | God in Man | 148 |
| Chap. V. | Of Divination | 154 |

### BOOK V.

| | | |
|---|---|---|
| Chap. I. | The Behaviour of a Philosopher | 156 |
| Chap. II. | On Habit | 159 |
| Chap. III. | On Disputation | 164 |
| Chap. IV. | That we should be Slow in Accepting Pleasure | 166 |
| Chap. V. | That we should be Open in our Dealings | 166 |
| Chap. VI. | That Half True may be all False | 167 |
| Chap. VII. | That each Man Play his Own Part | 167 |
| Chap. VIII. | That we should be Careful of the Soul as of the Body | 168 |
| Chap. IX. | The Measure of Gain | 168 |
| Chap. X. | The Worth of Women | 169 |
| Chap. XI. | A Dull Nature | 169 |
| Chap. XII. | Of Adornment of the Person | 170 |
| Chap. XIII. | Why we should Bear with Wrong | 174 |
| Chap. XIV. | That Everything hath Two Handles | 175 |
| Chap. XV. | On certain False Conclusions | 175 |
| Chap. XVI. | Perception and Judgment | 176 |
| Chap. XVII. | That the Philosopher shall Exhibit to the Vulgar Deeds, not Words | 179 |
| Chap. XVIII. | Ascesis | 180 |
| Chap. XIX. | Tokens | 181 |
| Chap. XX. | That the Logical Art is Necessary | 182 |
| Chap. XXI. | Grammarian or Sage | 183 |
| Chap. XXII. | Accomplishments | 184 |
| Chap. XXIII. | Constancy | 190 |
| Chap. XXIV. | How Long? | 190 |
| Chap. XXV. | Parts of Philosophy | 191 |
| Chap. XXVI. | Memorabilia | 192 |
| Notes | | 193 |
| Notes on the Principal Philosophic Terms used by Epictetus | | 215 |
| Index of References | | 219 |

" *Dass der Mensch ins Unvermeidliche sich füge, darauf dringen alle Religionen; jede sucht auf ihre Weise mit dieser Aufgabe fertig zu werden.*"
—GOETHE.

"——*Liber Epicteti nobilissimi Stoici.*"
—ST. AUGUSTINE.

# INTRODUCTION.

BUT for the zeal and ability of one disciple we should not now possess any trustworthy account of the teaching of Epictetus. For, like not a few other sages, he wrote nothing—his teaching was purely oral, delivered, in the form of lectures or discourses, to the students who came to him to receive their education in philosophy. One of these students was Flavius Arrianus, afterwards Senator and Consul of Rome, named by Lucian "one among the first of Roman men," and known to us chiefly as author of the best history of Alexander the Great which was produced in antiquity. That history is still extant, but posterity owes Arrian still more abundant thanks for the copious notes of the teaching of Epictetus which he took down from his master's lips in Nicopolis. This record he afterwards published in eight books (whereof only four now remain), entitled the *Dissertations of Epictetus;* and out of these he drew the materials for compiling the little work, the

*Encheiridion*, or Manual, of Epictetus, by which this philosopher has hitherto been most generally known.[1]

It is clear that the *Dissertations* were not regarded by Arrian as a satisfactory representation of the teaching of his master; that he published them, indeed, with much reluctance, and only when it appeared that unless he did so, certain imperfect versions of his records would be established as the sole sources of authoritative information about Epictetus. These circumstances are explained in a dedicatory letter to his friend Lucius Gellius, prefixed to the edition of the *Dissertations* which Arrian finally resolved to issue. I here translate this document in full:—

"Arrian to Lucius Gellius, hail.

"I did not write [in literary form and composition, συγγράφειν] the words of Epictetus in the manner in which a man might write such things. Neither have I put them forth among men, since, as I say, I did not even write them. But whatever I heard him speak, those things I endeavoured to set down in his very words, so to preserve to myself for future times a memorial of his thought and unstudied speech. Naturally, therefore, they are such things as one man might say to another on the occasion of

---

[1] *The Encheiridion of Epictetus*, Translated into English by T. W. Rolleston. Kegan Paul, Trench, & Co., 1881.

the moment, not such as he would put together with the idea of finding readers long afterwards. Such they are, and I know not how without my will or knowledge they fell among men. But to me it is no great matter if I shall appear unequal to composing such a work, and to Epictetus none at all if anyone shall despise his discourse; for when he spoke it, it was evident that he had but one aim—to stir the minds of his hearers towards the best things. And if, indeed, the words here written should do the same, then they will do, I think, that which the words of sages ought to do. But if not, yet let those who read them know this, that when he himself spoke them, it was impossible for the hearer to avoid feeling whatever Epictetus desired he should feel. But if his words, when they are merely words, have not this effect, perhaps it is that I am in fault, perhaps it could not have been otherwise. Farewell!"

The style of the *Dissertations*, as they have reached us, answers very well to the above account of their origin and purpose. They contain much that the world should be as little willing to neglect as anything that Greek philosophy has left us; but they contain also many repetitions, redundancies, incoherencies; and are absolutely devoid of any sort of order or system in their arrangement. Each chapter has generally something of a central theme, but beyond this all is chaos. The same theme will be dwelt on again and again in almost the same phrases; utterances of majestic wisdom are embedded in pages of tedious argument, and any grouping of the chapters according to a progressive sequence of ideas will be looked for in vain.

Under these conditions it was evident that the teaching of Epictetus could never win half the influence which its essential qualities fitted it to exercise. And accordingly, as another and better vehicle for this influence, Arrian compiled and condensed from the *Dissertations* the small handbook of the Stoic philosophy known as the *Encheiridion of Epictetus*. This little work has made Epictetus known to very many whom the *Dissertations* would never have reached. It had the distinction—unparalleled in the case of any other Pagan writing, if we except the doubtful *Sententiæ* of Xystus—of being adopted as a religious work in the early Christian Church. Two paraphrases of it—still extant—one of which was specially designed for the use of monastic bodies, were produced about the sixth century A.D., in which very few changes were made in the text, beyond the alteration of Pagan names and allusions to Scriptural ones.

About the same time it was made the subject of an elaborate and lengthy commentary by a pagan writer, Simplicius, wherein chapter after chapter is dissected, discussed, and explained. It was elegantly rendered into Latin by the well-known scholar of the Renaissance, Angelo Politian, who dedicated his translation to Lorenzo de' Medici. Down to the present day, as numerous translations testify, it has remained the most usual means of access to the thought of Epictetus.

But inestimable as the *Encheiridion* is, he who knows it alone has gained nothing like all that Epictetus has to give. It is a compendium; and although much more stirring and forcible than is usual with such works, it cannot give us the wealth of interesting allusion, reflection, humour, the bursts of eloquence, the abrupt and biting style, the vivid revelations of personal feeling, which marked the teaching of Epictetus in the form in which he delivered it. It seems, therefore, that to make him as accessible as he can be to those for whom such things have any value or interest, it were necessary to produce from the *Encheiridion* and the *Dissertations* a third work, which should have the advantages of each. This is what I have endeavoured to do in the present work. In it the whole of the *Encheiridion* is given, and the divisions of subject-matter into which the *Encheiridion* falls have been observed by the division of my translation into five Books, corresponding with the natural divisions of the *Encheiridion*—Book I., treating of the first principles of the Stoic philosophy; Book II., dealing with the general application of these principles to life; Book III., with man's relations to his fellow-man; Book IV., with his relations to God; Book V., containing, besides a couple of concluding chapters, chiefly practical counsels of behaviour on various particular occasions, and *obiter dicta* on the use of the faculties. Such is the scheme of arrangement suggested by the *Encheiridion*; and I have filled it in by setting among the chapters of the *Encheiridion* chapters or passages from the *Dissertations*, selected for their relevancy to the matter in hand. In fact, I have reversed the process by which the *Encheiridion* came into being. It was condensed out of the *Dissertations:* I have expanded it again by drawing into it a large quantity of material from the original work, and subjecting the new matter thus gained to the system and order of sequence which I found to prevail in the *Encheiridion*. The passages or chapters taken from the *Dissertations* are those which seemed to me most characteristic of the philosophy or the personality of Epictetus, and I have made it my aim to omit nothing which is essential to a full and clear understanding of the message he had to deliver to his generation. Of course there is plenty of room for differences of opinion as to the manner in which this conception

## INTRODUCTION.

has been here carried out; but I hope that the present attempt may do something to win a larger audience for his teaching than former editions could, in the nature of the case, obtain. If this hope should prove to be well founded, I shall expect, some day, to give the present English version a counterpart in a Greek text arranged on the same lines.

I may add here that the reader will find an Index at the end of this volume, in which every paragraph is referred to its original source in the *Dissertations, Encheiridion,* or *Fragments*—the references applying to Schweighäuser's standard edition of Epictetus.[1]

As regards the style of my translation, I hope the tinge of archaism I have given it will be felt to suit the matter. I could think of no idiom so varied, so flexible even down to its use of various grammatical forms,

---

[1] Epicteti Dissertationum ab Arriano Digestarum Libri IV. et ex Deperditis Sermonibus Fragmenta. Post Io. Uptoni aliorumque curas, denuo ad Codicum MStorum fidem recensuit, Latina Versione, Adnotationibus, Indicibus illustravit Johannes Schweighäuser. Lipsiæ. MDCCXCIX.

Epicteti Manuale et Cebetis Tabula Græce et Latine. Schw. MDCCXCVIII.

There are two excellent English translations of the whole extant works of Epictetus—one by Mrs. Carter, published in the last century, the other by the late George Long, M.A. (Bohn Series), to both of which, but especially the latter, I desire to record my great obligations.

so well suited alike to colloquy, or argument, or satire, or impassioned eloquence as Elizabethan English.

So much to make the plan of the present work understood; and the reader may perhaps wish that I would now leave him to the study of it. But there is much in Epictetus the significance of which will not appear to anyone who is unacquainted with the general system of Stoic philosophy which formed the basis of Epictetus's ethical teaching. And I hope that the reader will prefer to have such information as is necessary given him in the form of a general introduction rather than in that of a multitude of notes.

The founder of the Stoic philosophy was Zeno, a native of Cyprus, who taught in Athens, about 300 B.C., in that frescoed arcade, or Stoa, which gave its name to his school. His birth-place is worth noting, for Zeno lived at the beginning of that epoch, himself one of the first products of it, in which the influence of the East became strongly apparent in Greek thought; the period called Hellenistic in contradistinction to the purely Hellenic period which ended in the conquests of the Macedonians. In many ways the conditions of life in the Hellenistic period formed the most favourable *milieu* possible for the development of Greek thought upon the only lines which, after Aristotle, it could fruitfully pursue; and this not in spite of, but even because of, the great

## INTRODUCTION.

degradation of political and social life from which all Hellendom then suffered. What the democratic polities were like, on which was laid the problem of confronting Philip of Macedon, we may conjecture from the history of the best known and assuredly not the worst of them, Athens. And the best type of Athenian whose rise to power was favoured by the conditions of this time and place was Demosthenes: Demosthenes, the grand historical warning to all peoples against committing their destinies to professional orators; the statesman whose doubtless real veneration for his country and her past served only to make him a more mischievous counsellor in her present difficulties; whose splendid power as a wielder of words was scarcely more signal than his incapacity and cowardice when he was called upon to match those words with deeds. Athens, entangling the Thebans in an alliance against Macedon, and then leaving them to face Alexander alone; deifying Demetrius the Besieger for driving out a Macedonian garrison, and allotting him the Parthenon itself to be his lodging and the scene of his unspeakable profligacies; murdering Phocion, the one man who dared to bring sincerity and virtue to her service —Athens was a type of the Greek States of this epoch: too unprincipled for democratic government, too contentious for despotism, too vain to submit to

*b*

foreign rule, too lacking in valour, purpose, union, to resist it with effect.

Whatever the causes of the change may have been, the conditions of public life in this Hellenistic period were certainly very different from those which prevailed, albeit with decadence, before that vast breaking up of boundaries and destruction of political systems involved in the Macedonian conquests. The successful and inspiring conflict with Persia waged by the Hellenic States had for a time made all Greek hearts to beat with one aspiration, and had brought to the front a race of leaders who were capable of subduing the Greek democracies to their own steadfast and statesmanlike purposes. Public life was then not only a possible but even the most natural career for a man of talent and probity. The small size of the Greek States gave almost every such man an opportunity of action, and so keen and universal was the interest in politics that it threatened to lead Greek philosophy into a region in which philosophy is very apt to lose its vitalising connection with human consciousness and experience, and to stiffen into barren speculation. In a word, man, as an individual, began to be too much lost sight of in the consideration of man as a citizen; his uses, his duties, the whole worth and significance of his life, came to be estimated too exclusively by his relations to the visible society about him. It was when the great Stoic Chrysippus found himself obliged to stand aloof from all participation in politics—" For if I counsel honourably I shall offend the citizens, and if basely, the Gods"—that such men as he were led to ask themselves: Is there then any sphere of human endeavour out of the reach of the tyranny of circumstance? If I cannot be a citizen, what am I worth then simply as a man? If I can be nothing to my fellows, what can I be to God? To a state of things, then, which, speaking broadly, made public life impossible to honest men, we owe the noblest ethical system of antiquity; to the enforced concentration of thought upon the individual we owe a certain note of universality till then absent from Hellenic thought.

But Stoicism was not the only product of the speculation of this period. Side by side with it there started into being two other systems of philosophy, the necessity for combating which was doubtless of immense service to its development. These were Epicureanism and Pyrrhonism; and as the reader will find Epictetus much concerned with each of them, it may be desirable that I should give some brief account of their cardinal doctrines.

Epicurus was an Athenian. After some residence in Lesbos and Lampsacus, he began to teach in his native city about the year 306 B.C. His ethical views, which are all that concern us here, were of a distinctly unelevating nature. Pleasure, ἡδονή, was pronounced to be for each man the end and aim of his being, and the only rational motive of action. This, however, was not the pleasure of the voluptuary— its highest forms, according to Epicurus, were gained in ἀταραξία and ἀπονία—that is, a cheerful and unanxious temperament, with leisure for contemplation, ends not attainable by the criminal who lives in constant fear of detection, or the luxurious liver in whom satiety produces disgust and weariness.

Certain bodily conditions were, however, regarded as objects in themselves, and partaking of the nature of the absolutely good; and all entanglement in human relationships was discountenanced for the disturbance and distress which such relationships were liable to cause. These doctrines were put in practice by their teacher in inuring himself to a hermit-like simplicity and abstemiousness of life; and his life was philosophically consistent with his doctrines, for it is clear that the end of Pleasure will be most surely gained by him who has fewest wants to gratify. But though the lives of Epicurus and his immediate followers were exceptionally sober and strict, the total effect of his doctrines could not but have been evil. They were purely egoistic in this

## INTRODUCTION.    xxi

tendency—they centred each man's activity and interest upon himself alone, they bade him take no thought for any other earthly or heavenly thing, and taught him that this ideal of indifference was realised in its full perfection by the Gods, who dwelt apart in divine repose while blind necessity had its way with human destiny.

Pyrrho of Elis, a rather earlier teacher than Zeno or Epicurus, who is said to have studied philosophy under Indian Gymnosophists and Chaldean Magi, was the originator in European thought of a great and permanent philosophic movement. His school was inspired by the *Geist der stets verneint*, and the term Sceptic was first devised to describe its attitude. Its strength is in a discovery which inevitably takes place when men begin to reflect upon their own mental operations—the discovery, namely, that, given a perceiving mind and a perceived object, it is always possible for the former, if it has the power of introspection, to doubt whether it has received a really true and faithful impression of the latter. How can we be assured that external objects are as we perceive them? How can we even be assured that there is any principle of constancy in their relations to our consciousness? The senses often delude us; we are convinced, in dreams, of the reality of appearances which, nevertheless, have no reality—why may not all perception be a delusion? Why may not even our sense of the validity of inference and of the truth of the axioms of geometry be a pure hallucination? With these searching questions the Sceptic cut at the root of all belief, and the problems which they raise have dominated philosophy down to the present day. Nor in two thousand years has any logical answer to them ever been found. Lotze, the last thinker of really first-rate powers that the world has seen, practically abandons all inquiry into theories of perception, and starts with the *assumption* that we are living in a kosmos, not a chaos; that the order, coherence, reason in things to which consciousness testifies, are realities. In antiquity, I may add, the profound problems raised by Pyrrhonism do not seem to have been very profoundly apprehended either by the Pyrrhonists or their opponents. The latter had nothing better to appeal to than that notoriously feeble resource, the *argumentum ad hominem*. If the Pyrrhonist distrusted the evidence of his senses, they asked, why did he avoid walking over precipices or into the sea, or eat bread instead of earth, or in any way make choice of means for ends? The Pyrrhonist's answer was equally superficial. It anticipated the famous formula of Bishop Butler. Probability, argued they, was the guide of life— having observed certain results to follow from certain antecedents, the prudent man will shape his course in life accordingly, although, as a matter of theory and speculation, he may refuse to believe in the constancy of nature. This answer involves a clear inconsistency. It involves even a greater assumption than that which the Pyrrhonist refused to make as to the credibility of his perceptions—the assumption of the credibility of his recollections. To the thoroughgoing Sceptic there is no such thing as past experience —he is, as it were, new-born at each instant of his life.

Such, in outline, were the systems against which the Stoic philosophy had to make good its position in the ancient world. From the first there seems to have been no doubt of its ability to do so, although, unhappily, the records which have been preserved of the teaching of its earliest days are few and obscure. The writings of Zeno, the founder of Stoicism, and of Chrysippus, his immediate successor in the leadership of the school, have utterly perished, while of Cleanthes, the third of the early Stoic teachers, very little remains beyond the profound and majestic Hymn to Zeus, of which I have given a translation in this work. The complete loss of the hundreds of treatises produced by Chrysippus is especially to be regretted, as he appears to have taken the main part in giving shape and system to the Stoic philosophy. "Had Chrysippus not been, the Stoa had not been," was a proverbial saying which testifies to his fame. However, from the accounts of ancient philosophers in Diogenes Läertius, from Plutarch, Seneca, Cicero, and a few other authorities, we can learn pretty clearly what the framework of the Stoic system had grown to be long before Epictetus began to study it.

In antiquity, a philosophic system was expected to have something to say for itself on three different branches of study—Logic, Physics (which included cosmogony and theology), and Ethics. We think of the Stoics chiefly in connection with the last-named of these subjects, but they were no less eminent in the others, and Chrysippus, in particular, was held to have done so much for the science of logic that a saying was current—"If there were dialectic among the Gods, it must be the dialectic of Chrysippus." Of the Stoic contributions to this science, scarcely any record remains.

Of their physical system, however, much is known, and the reader of Epictetus needs to be acquainted with its general features. These were borrowed from an earlier thinker, Heracleitus, whose central doctrine was that the universe was an eternal flux and transition; everything was in a state of becoming, *ein Werdendes*. At the beginning of things, so far as they can be said to have any beginning, is the Deity in

## INTRODUCTION.

his purest manifestation, which, be it observed, is a strictly material one, a sublimated and ethereal fire, αἰθερῶδες πῦρ. In this fire dwelt the divine creative thought and impulse. The first step in that process of differentiation in which development consists is the production of vapour, which condensed into water. Two elementary forces play their part in these operations—a movement towards within, and a movement towards without, the one a densifying, the other an expanding and straining force (τόνος). The former gives us solidity in matter, the other the qualities and energies of matter. Thus, by various degrees of density, we get earth, water, atmospheric air, and from air, the common element of earthly fire ; and these elements in their various combinations, with their various attributes and powers, gradually produce the successive stages of organic life. Though all these proceed from the substance of the Divine Being, the Stoics recognised, in the derived substances which make up the universe as we have it now, various degrees of purity, of affinity to their original source. Man's body, for instance, with its passions and affections, lies comparatively far from the divine; but his soul is a veritable ray of the primitive fire, *Deus in corpore humano hospitans.* The popular mythology of the day was entirely rejected by the Stoics, although, as Professor Mahaffy points out, they never attempted to "discredit orthodoxy," but, on the contrary, used its myths and ceremonies with the utmost reverence as vehicles of profound religious truths. But they certainly believed in intelligences above man, yet below the one Supreme Being; thus the stars and the lightning (the reader will observe the allusions in the Hymn of Cleanthes) are in some sense divinities, by virtue of the supposed purity of their fiery essence.

Thus from the one primitive divine element the Kosmos, with all its hierarchy of being, is evolved. But in the Stoic system πάντα ῥεῖ,[1] there is no continuance in any one condition. As in the normal life of all earthly creatures there comes a certain climax or turning point, after which the forces of decay gain slowly but surely on those of growth and resistance, so also runs the history of the universe which includes them all. One by one the steps by which it was formed shall be retraced, and the derived substances which compose it consumed and re-absorbed by that from which they sprang. From matter in its grossest form to its purest, from earth and stone and water to the highest intelligence in men and dæmons and Gods, nothing shall escape this doom of dissolution; everything shall yield up its separate

---

[1] πάντα ῥεῖ, all flows—the cardinal doctrine of the Heracleitean philosophy.

## INTRODUCTION.

existence, until at last the indestructible element of that primæval fire is again the sole being that remains, and Zeus is "alone in the conflagration," self-contemplating in the solitudes of thought. But this is not the end. There is no end. The plastic impulse again resumes its sway, and soon another cycle of world-development and world-destruction begins to run its course. In the language of Seneca, "When that fatal day, that necessity of the times, shall have arrived, and it seems good to God to make an end of old things and ordain the better, then shall the ancient order be revoked and every creature be generated anew, and a race ignorant of guilt be given to the earth."

This was the general physical system on which all Stoics were agreed, although there were differences of opinion upon minor points; such as how far these successive cycles resembled each other? some asserting that they did so in the minutest detail, others only in their larger features. It was a system, for all its superstitions, not without grandeur and truth. At bottom it expressed a sense of that phenomenon of ebb and flow, systole and diastole, the action and counteraction of balanced forces, which is perhaps the profoundest law of life.

Two questions arise in connection with the Stoic cosmogony, which we must briefly discuss before proceeding farther. Are we justified in terming their view of the universe a materialistic one? and what was their doctrine of the destinies of the human soul? Now it is certainly the usual practice among writers on philosophy to reckon the Stoics as materialists, and it is unquestionably true that they denied the possibility of any existence which was not corporeal. Strong as they are on the supremacy of the human soul over the human body, sharp as is the line with which they divide these elements, yet the distinction is a moral, not a metaphysical one—each is an actual material substance. But we shall be seriously mistaken, nevertheless, if we place them in the same class with the scientific materialists of the present day. According to the latter, Thought is no necessary moment in the universe, but merely a product of certain accidental combinations of matter, a product which, when these are dissolved, must disappear from existence, without leaving a trace of its presence behind. Again, according to most modern opponents of the materialistic view, Thought has an independent and immortal being—it existed before matter was, and would continue to exist if all matter were annihilated. The Stoic view differed from each of these modern theories. It held Thought and Matter to be eternal, inseparable, and, indeed, strictly identical. Being in its primitive and purest form was Fire, a corporeal substance, but one exhibiting consciousness, purpose, will.

As to the question of the Stoic view of the immortality of the human soul, it does not seem to me to deserve so much discussion as it has received from some commentators. It is obvious that the soul must, in the end, share the lot of all other existences, and be resolved into the Divine Being which was its source. The only question that can arise is whether this resolution takes place at the moment of death, or whether the sense of personal identity persists for a certain period beyond that event; and this question, which Epictetus appears to have been wise enough to leave an open one, is philosophically of very little importance. The soul is immortal, the individual perishes; this is the conclusion of Stoicism, and if we know this, there is little else it can much concern us to know.

The reader who desires to gain a thorough knowledge of Hellenistic philosophy, and of the social and political conditions in which it throve, will find what he seeks in two works to which I have to express my large indebtedness. One is Zeller's *Philosophie der Griechen (Epikureer, Stoiker u. Skeptiker)*[1], a monument of German research and erudition, in which vast masses of original material for the study

---

[1] An English translation of this work has lately appeared.

of this most interesting, but neglected, epoch of the development of European intellect have been brought together, and interpreted with more than German lucidity and method. The other is Professor Mahaffy's recent volume, *Greek Life and Thought*, a study of the Hellenistic period in various aspects, which the scholar will not read without profit, nor the lay-reader without pleasure.

We turn now to that department of the Stoic philosophy with which the reader of Epictetus is most concerned—its Ethics.

The ethical question resolves itself into a search for the supreme object of human endeavour, the *Summum Bonum*, the absolute and essential good. This, for the Stoic, embodied itself in the formula, "to live according to Nature." But what is Nature? The will of God, as revealed in the heart and conscience of those who seek to know it, and interpreted through the observation in a reverent and faithful spirit of the facts of life.

Going into the subject more precisely we find certain criteria of moral truth established, προλήψεις, as they were called, that is, primitive, original conceptions, or, as I have rendered them in my translation, "natural conceptions," dogmas by which all moral questions can be tried. If we inquire into the source of these προλήψεις, we shall find ourselves

## INTRODUCTION. xxxi

mistaken in our disposition to think that the Stoics regarded them as innate ideas. Innate they are not, for the Stoics held the soul at birth to be a *tabula rasa*, or blank page, which only experience could fill with character and meaning. But as Seneca says in his inquiry, "Quomodo ad nos prima boni honestique notitia pervenerit,"[1] although Nature alone could not teach us these things, could not equip us with the knowledge of them before we entered upon life, yet the "seeds" of this knowledge she does give us; the soul of every man has implanted in it a certain aptness or, indeed, necessity to deduce certain universal truths from such observation and experience as are common to all mankind; and these truths, the προλήψεις, though not strictly innate, have thus an inevitableness and dogmatic force not possessed by those which one man may reach and another miss in the exercise of the ordinary faculties, by argument, study, and so forth. By these natural conceptions the existence and character of God, and the general decrees of the moral law, are considered to be affirmed. If we inquire further how the Stoic explained the fact that some of these so-called inevitable and universal conclusions are denied in all sincerity by men like Epicurus, who were neither bad nor mad, we strike

---

[1] Ep. 120. 4. ff.

upon the difficulty which confronts all systems that aim at setting up any absolute body of truth, expressible in human language, in place of that partial, progressive, and infinitely varied revelation of God's mind and purpose to which the uncoloured facts of the world's religious history seem to testify.

The natural conceptions, as I have said, contain the primary doctrines of ethics. None of these are more important for the Stoic than that which declares essential Good to lie in the active, not the passive side of man; in the will, not in the flesh, nor in anything else which the will is unable to control. But a certain relative and conditional goodness may lie in matters which are yet of no moment to the spiritual man, to that part of him which seeks the essential good. And we must note that when Epictetus speaks of certain things as good or bad or indifferent, he is generally speaking of them in their relation to the spiritual man, and in the most absolute and unconditional sense. No evil can happen to the essential part of man, to that side of him which is related to the eternal and divine, without his own will. Hence the death of a beloved friend, or child, or wife, is no evil; and if it be no evil, we are forbidden to grieve for it, or, in the most usual phrase with Epictetus, we are not to be troubled. or confounded by it, ταράσσεσθαι. But if this utterance should shock our natural feelings, it will do something which assuredly Epictetus never meant it to do. It is the soul of man which these events cannot injure, and it is the soul which is forbidden to think itself injured by them. Such love of the individual as may be embraced in the larger love of the All, of God—such grief for bereavements and calamities as does not overwhelm the inner man (ii. 19) in a " wave of mortal tumult," and dull his vital sense of the great moral ends which he was born to pursue, is repeatedly and explicitly admitted by Epictetus. Thus, in iii. 2, we have him arguing against Epicurus that there are certain natural sympathies between man and his kind, and even convicting Epicurus himself of a secret belief in these sympathies. Epicurus had dissuaded his followers from marriage, and the bringing-up of children, on account of the grief and anxiety which such relations necessarily entail. Not so the Stoics—they pressed their disciples to enter into the ordinary earthly relationships of husband, or wife, or citizen, and this without pretending to have found any means of averting the natural consequences which Epicurus dreaded, although they did profess to have discovered something in man which made him equal to the endurance of them. . Again, although the condition of $\mathring{a}\pi\mathring{a}\theta\epsilon\iota a$ of inward peace, of freedom from passions, is again and again represented by Epictetus as the mark of the perfect sage, we are told that this ἀπάθεια is something quite different from "apathy"—a man is not to be emotionless "like a statue." And a third passage confirming this view is to be found in Book I., ch. xi. (Schweighäuser), where the conduct of a man who was so afflicted by the illness of his little daughter that he ran away from the house, and would hear news of her only through messages, is condemned, not for the affection and anxiety it proved, but for its utter unreasonableness. "Would you," asks Epictetus, "have her mother and her nurse and her pedagogue, who all love her too, also run away from her, and leave her to die in the hands of persons who neither love nor care for her at all?" There is a grief which is really a self-indulgence, a barren, absorbing, paralysing grief, which, to the soul possessed by it, makes every other thing in heaven and earth seem strange and cold and trivial. From such grief alone Epictetus would deliver us, and I think he would have accepted Mr. Aubrey de Vere's noble sonnet on *Sorrow* as a thoroughly fit poetic statement of Stoic doctrine on this subject:—

"Count each affliction, whether light or grave,
  God's messenger sent down to thee ; do thou
  With courtesy receive him ; rise and bow ;
  And, ere his shadow pass thy threshold, crave
  Permission first his heavenly feet to lave ;

Then lay before him all thou hast, allow
No cloud of passion to usurp thy brow,
Or mar thy hospitality; no wave
Of mortal tumult to obliterate
The soul's marmoreal calmness: Grief should be
Like joy, majestic, equable, sedate;
Confirming, cleansing, raising, making free;
Strong to consume small troubles; to commend
Great thoughts, grave thoughts, thoughts lasting to the end."

But the grief that shall do this is a grief that must be *felt*. And Epictetus assuredly never meant to offer the Stoic philosophy as a mere stupefying anodyne. Make the man a Stoic, and something yet remains to do—to make the Stoic a man. One of these purposes was not more the concern of Epictetus than the other. And he pursued both of them with a strength, sincerity, and sanity of thought, with a power of nourishing the heroic fibre in humanity, which, to my mind, make him the very chief of Pagan moralists.

It is no purpose of mine to fill this preface with information which the reader can gain without doubt or difficulty from the author whom it introduces, and therefore I shall leave him to discover for himself what the positive ethical teaching of Epictetus was like. Nor is it, unhappily, possible to say much upon another subject on which Epictetus gives us little or no information—his own life and circumstances. Arrian wrote a biography of him, but it is now entirely lost, and the biographical details which have been collected from Simplicius, Suidas, Aulus Gellius, and others are very scanty. He was born at Hierapolis, in Phrygia, and became, how is unknown, a slave of Epaphroditus, a freedman and favourite of Nero, who is recorded to have treated him with great cruelty. One day, it is said, Epaphroditus began twisting his leg for amusement. Epictetus said, "If you go on you will break my leg." Epaphroditus persisted, the leg was broken, and Epictetus, with unruffled serenity, only said, "Did I not tell you that you would break my leg?" This circumstance is adduced by Celsus in his famous controversy with Origen as an instance of Pagan fortitude equal to anything which Christian martyrology had to show;[1] but it is probably a mere myth which grew up to account for the fact mentioned by Simplicius and Suidas that Epictetus was feeble in body and lame from an early age.

Epaphroditus was probably a very bad master, and as a favourite and intimate of Nero's, must have been

---

[1] Gregory Nazianzen, commenting on this narrative, remarks that it only shows how manfully *unavoidable* sufferings may be borne.

## INTRODUCTION. xxxvii

a bad man; but we have to thank him for the fact that Epictetus, while yet a slave, was sent to attend the philosophic lectures of Musonius Rufus, an eminent Stoic of Rome, whom both Epictetus and Marcus Aurelius mention with great respect. The system of philosophic training had been at this time long organised. There were masters of repute everywhere, who delivered their instruction in regular courses, received a fixed payment for the same, and under whom crowds of young men assembled from far and near to study science and ethics—to receive, in short, what corresponded to a university education in those days. The curious circumstance that a slave like Epictetus could participate in advantages of this kind is generally explained as the result of a fashionable whim which possessed Roman nobles at this time for having philosophers and men of culture among their slaves. Professor Mahaffy, in his *Greek Life and Thought* (p. 132), commenting on the summons of the two philosophers, Anaxarchus and Callisthenes, to console Alexander after his murder of Cleitus, observes that it was probably usual to call in philosophers to minister professionally in cases of affliction. From this, to making a philosopher a regular adjunct to a large household, even as the baron of later times kept a fool, the step is not great. But Epaphroditus, one thinks, must have had frequent reason to rue the choice he made in Epictetus, if he expected his domestic philosopher to excuse his misdeeds as Anaxarchus did those of Alexander on the occasion above mentioned.

In the year 94 A.D. the emperor Domitian issued a decree expelling all philosophers from Rome—an easily explainable proceeding on his part if there were any large number of them who, in the words of Epictetus, were able "to look tyrants steadily in the face." Epictetus must have by this time obtained his freedom and set up for himself as a professor of philosophy, for we find him, in consequence of this decree, betaking himself to Nicopolis, a city of Epirus. Here he lived and taught to a venerable age, and here he delivered the discourses which Arrian has reported for us. He lived with great simplicity, and is said to have had no servant or other inmate of his house until he hired a nurse for an infant which was about to be exposed, according to the practice of those days when it was desired to check the inconvenient growth of a family, and which Epictetus rescued and brought up. The date of his death is unknown.

And now, reader, I will take my leave of you with Arrian's farewell salutation to Lucius Gellius, which, literally translated, is *Be strong*. If you need it, I know no teacher better able to make or keep you so than Epictetus. At any rate, to give him a fair chance of doing what it is in him to do for English-speaking men and women is something I have regarded as a sort of duty, a discharge of obligation for his infinite service to myself; which done to the utmost of my powers, the fewest forewords are the best.

T. W. R.

# CLEANTHES' HYMN TO ZEUS.[1]

Most glorious of the Immortals, many named, Almighty for ever.
Zeus, ruler of Nature, that governest all things with law,
Hail! for lawful it is that all mortals should address Thee.
For we are Thy offspring, taking the image only of Thy voice,[2] as many mortal things as live and move upon the earth.
Therefore will I hymn Thee, and sing Thy might forever.
For Thee doth all this universe that circles round the earth obey, moving whithersoever Thou leadest, and is gladly swayed by Thee,
Such a minister hast Thou in Thine invincible hands;—the two-edged, blazing, imperishable thunderbolt.
For under its stroke all Nature shuddereth, and by it thou guidest aright the Universal Reason, that roams through all things, mingling itself with the greater and the lesser lights, till it have grown so great, and become supreme king over all.
Nor is aught done on the earth without Thee, O God, nor in the divine sphere of the heavens, nor in the sea,
Save the works that evil men do in their folly—
Yea, but Thou knowest even to find a place for superfluous things, and to order that which is disorderly, and things not dear to men are dear to Thee.

---
[1] See notes on the Hymn of Cleanthes.

Thus dost Thou harmonise into One all good and evil things, that there should be one everlasting Reason of them all.

And this the evil among mortal men avoid and heed not; wretched, ever desiring to possess the good, yet they nor see nor hear the universal Law of God, which obeying with all their heart, their life would be well.

But they rush graceless each to his own aim,

Some cherishing lust for fame, the nurse of evil strife,

Some bent on monstrous gain,

Some turned to folly and the sweet works of the flesh,

Hastening, indeed, to bring the very contrary of these things to pass.

But Thou, O Zeus, the All-giver, Dweller in the darkness of cloud, Lord of thunder, save Thou men from their unhappy folly,

Which do Thou, O Father, scatter from their souls; and give them to discover the wisdom, in whose assurance Thou governest all things with justice;

So that being honoured, they may pay Thee honour,

Hymning Thy works continually, as it beseems a mortal man.

Since there can be no greater glory for men or Gods than this,

Duly to praise for ever the Universal Law.

# THE TEACHING OF EPICTETUS.

## BOOK I.

### CHAPTER I.

THE BEGINNING OF PHILOSOPHY.

1. WOULDST thou be good, then first believe that thou art evil.

2. The beginning of philosophy, at least with those who lay hold of it as they ought and enter by the door,[1] is the consciousness of their own feebleness and incapacity in respect of necessary things.

3. For we come into the world having by nature no idea of a right-angled triangle, or a quarter-tone, or a semi-tone, but by a certain tradition of art we learn each of these things. And thus those who know them not, do not suppose that they know them. But good and evil, and nobleness and baseness, and the seemly and the unseemly, and happiness and misfortune, and what is our concern and what is not, and

---

[1] See *Notes*, Bk. 1., ch. i. 1. The small numerals in the text refer throughout to the Notes at the end of the volume; each chapter having, where notes are necessary, its own chapter of Notes.

what ought to be done and what not—who hath come into the world without an implanted notion of these things? Thus we all use these terms, and endeavour to fit our natural conceptions to every several thing. *He did well, rightly, not rightly, he failed, he succeeded, he is unrighteous, he is righteous* —which of us spareth to use terms like these? Which of us will defer the use of them till he hath learned them, even as ignorant men do not use terms of geometry or music? But this is the reason of it: we come into the world already, as it were, taught by Nature some things in this kind, and setting out from these things we have added thereto our own conceit.² *For how*, saith one, *do I not know what is noble and what is base? Have I not the notion of it?* Truly. *And do I not apply it to things severally?* You do apply it. *Do I not, then, apply it rightly?* But here lies the whole question, and here conceit entereth in. For setting out from things confessed by all they go on by a false application to that which is disputed. For if, in addition to those things, they had gained also this power of application, what would then hinder them to be perfect? But now since you think that you apply rightly the natural conceptions to things severally, tell me, whence have you this assurance?

———" Because it seems so to me."

But to another it seems otherwise—and he, too, doth he think his application right or not?

———" He doth think it."

Can ye, then, both be rightly applying the con-

## THE BEGINNING OF PHILOSOPHY. 5

ceptions in matters wherein your opinions contradict each other.

—" We cannot."

Have you, then, aught better to show for your application, or aught above this, that it seemeth so to you? But what else doth a madman do, than those things that to him seem right? And doth this rule suffice for him?

—" It doth not suffice."

Come, then, to that which is above seeming. What is this?

4. Behold, the beginning of philosophy is the observation of how men contradict each other, and the search whence cometh this contradiction, and the censure and mistrust of bare opinion. And it is an inquiry into that which seems, whether it rightly seems; and the discovery of a certain rule, even as we have found a balance for weights, and a plumb line for straight and crooked. This is the beginning of philosophy. Are all things right to all to whom they seem so? But how can contradictory things be right?

—" Nay, then, not all things, but those that seem to us right."

And why to you more than the Syrians, or to the Egyptians? Why more than to me or to any other man. Not at all more. Seeming, then, doth not for every man answer to Being; for neither in weights or measures doth the bare appearance content us, but for each case we have discovered some rule. And here, then, is there no rule above seeming? And how could it be that there were no evidence or discovery of things the most necessary for men? There is, then, a rule. And wherefore do we not seek it, and find it, and, having found it, henceforth use it without transgression, and not so much as stretch forth a finger without it? For this it is, I think, that when it is discovered cureth of their madness those that mismeasure all things by seeming alone; so that henceforth, setting out from things known and investigated, we may use an organised body of natural conceptions in all our several dealings.

5. What is the subject about which we are inquiring? Pleasure? Submit it to the rule, cast it into the scales. Now the Good must be a thing of such sort that we ought to trust in it? *Truly.* And we ought to have faith in it? *We ought.* And ought we to trust in anything which is unstable? *Nay.* And hath pleasure any stability? *It hath not.* Take it then, and fling it out of the scales, and set it far away from the place of the Good. But if you are dim of sight, and one balance doth not suffice, then take another. Is it right to be elated in what is good? *Yea.* And is it right to be elated then in the presence of a pleasure? See to it that thou say not it is right; or I shall not hold thee worthy even of the balance.[3] Thus are things judged and weighed, when the rules are held in readiness. And the aim of philosophy is this, to examine and establish the rules. And to use them when they are known is the task of an wise and good man.

## CHAPTER II.

### ON THE NATURAL CONCEPTIONS.

1. THE natural conceptions are common to all men, and one cannot contradict another. For which of us but affirms that the Good is profitable, and that we should choose it, and in all circumstances follow and pursue it? Which of us but affirms that uprightness is honourable and becoming? Where, then, doth the contradiction arise? Concerning the application of the natural conceptions to things severally. When one saith, *He did well, he is a worthy man*, and another, *Nay, but he did foolishly*, then there is a contradiction among men, one with another. And there is the same contradiction among the Jews and the Syrians and the Egyptians and the Romans; not whether that which is righteous should be preferred to all things and in all cases pursued, but whether this be righteous or unrighteous, to eat the flesh of swine. And ye can discover the same contradiction in the matter of Achilles and Agamemnon. For call them before us: What sayest thou, Agamemnon, Should not that which is right and fair come to pass?
—— " That should it."

And what sayest thou, Achilles, Doth it not please thee that what is fair and right should be done?
—— " Of all things this doth most please me."

Then make application of your natural conceptions. Whence arose this dispute? The one saith: *I am not bound to deliver up Chryseis to her father.* And the other saith: *Thou art bound.* Assuredly one of them must ill apply the conception of duty. And again the one saith: *Therefore if I should deliver up Chryseis, it is meet that I take his prize from one of you.* And the other: *Wouldst thou, then, take from me my beloved?* He saith: *Yea, even thine. And shall I alone, and I alone, have nothing?* And thus ariseth the contradiction.

2. What is it, then, to be educated? It is to learn to apply the natural conceptions to each thing severally according to nature; and further, to discern that of things that exist some are in our own power[1] and the rest are not in our own power. And things that are in our own power are the will, and all the works of the will. And things that are not in our own power are the body, and the parts of the body, and possessions and parents and brethren and children and country and, in a word, our associates. Where now shall we place the Good? To what objects shall we apply it? To those which are in our own power? Then is health not good, and whole limbs and life? and are not children and parents and country? And who will bear with you if you say this? Let us, then, transfer it to these things. Now, can one be happy who is injured, and has missed gaining what is good? He cannot. And can such a one bear himself towards his fellows as he ought? How is it possible that he should? For I have it of nature that I must seek my own profit. If it profits me to own a piece of land, it profits me to take it from

my neighbour. If it profits me to have a garment, it profits me to steal it from the bath. And hence wars, seditions, tyrannies, conspiracies. And how shall I be able to maintain a right mind towards God? for if I suffer injury and misfortune, it cannot be but He neglects me. And what have I to do with Him if He cannot help me? And, again, what have I to do with Him if he is willing to let me continue in the evils in which I am? Henceforth I begin to hate Him. Why, then, do we build temples and set up statues to Zeus as we do to powers of evil, such as Fever?[2] And how is He now the Saviour and the Raingiver and the Fruitgiver? And verily, all this follows, if we place anywhere in external things the nature and being of the Good.

## CHAPTER III.

#### THE MASTER-FACULTY.

1. OF all our faculties ye shall find but one that can contemplate itself, or, therefore, approve or disapprove itself. How far hath grammar the power of contemplation? Only so far as to judge concerning letters. And music? Only so far as to judge concerning melodies. Doth any of them, then, contemplate itself? Not one. But when you have need to write to your friend, grammar will tell you how to

write; but whether to write or not, grammar will not tell. And so with the musical art in the case of melodies; but whether it is now meet or not to sing or to play, music will not tell. What, then, will tell it? That faculty which both contemplates itself and all other things. And what is this? It is the faculty of Reason; for we have received none other which can consider itself—what it is, and what it can, and what it is worth—and all the other faculties as well. For what else is it that tells us that a golden thing is beautiful, since itself doth not? Clearly it is the faculty which makes use of appearances. What else is it that judges of music and grammar, and the other faculties, and proves their uses, and shows the fit occasions? None else than this.

2. Thus the Gods, as it was fit they should, place that only in our power which is the mightiest and master thing, the right use of appearances; but other things are not in our power. Was it that they did not wish it? I indeed think that had they been able they had made over to us those things also; but this they could in no way do. For being on the earth, and bound up with this flesh and with these associates, how was it possible that as regards these we should not be hindered by external things? But what saith Zeus? "Epictetus, if it were possible, I would have made both this thy little body and thy little property free and unhampered. But forget not now that this is but finely tempered clay, and nothing of thine own. And since I could not do this, I have given thee a part of ourselves, this power of desiring and

disliking, and pursuing, avoiding, and rejecting, and, in brief, the use of appearances. Have a care, then, of this, hold this only for thine own, and thou shalt never be hindered or hampered, thou shalt not lament, thou shalt not blame, thou shalt never flatter any man." What then? Do these seem trifling matters? *God forbid.* Are you, then, not content with them? *At least I pray the Gods I may be.*[1]

3. But now having one thing in our power to care for, and to cleave to, we rather choose to be careful of many things, and to bind ourselves to many things, even to the flesh, and to possessions, and to brother and friend and child and slave. And being thus bound to many things, they lie heavy on us and drag us down. So, if the weather be not fair for sailing, we sit down distraught and are ever peering forth to see how stands the wind. *It is north.* And what is that to us? *When will the west wind blow?* When it shall seem good to it, friend; or to Aeolus. For it was not thee, but Aeolus whom God made "steward of the winds."[2] What then? It is right to devise how we may perfect the things that are our own, and to use the others as their nature is. And what, then, is their nature? As it may please God.

## CHAPTER IV.

#### THE NATURE OF THE GOOD.

1. THE subject for the good and wise man is his own master-faculty, as the body is for the physician and the trainer, and the soil is the subject for the husbandman. And the work of the good and wise man is to use appearances according to Nature. For it is the nature of every soul to consent to what is good and to reject what is evil, and to hold back about what is uncertain; and thus to be moved to pursue the good and to avoid the evil, and neither way towards what is neither good nor evil. For as it is not lawful for the money-changer or the seller of herbs to reject Cæsar's coin, but if one present it, then, whether he will or no, he must give up what is sold for it, so it is also with the soul. When the Good appears, straightway the soul is moved towards it, and from the Evil. And never doth the soul reject any clear appearance of the good, no more than Cæsar's coin. On this hangeth every movement both of God and man.

2. The nature and essence of the Good is in a certain disposition of the Will; likewise that of the Evil. What, then, are outward things? Matter for the Will, about which being occupied it shall attain its own good or evil. How shall it attain the Good? Through not being dazzled with admiration of what it works on.[1] For our opinions of this, when right, make the

will right, and when wrong make it evil. This law hath God established, and saith, "If thou wouldst have aught of good, have it from thyself."

3. If these things are true (and if we are not fools or hypocrites), that Good, for man, lies in the Will, and likewise Evil, and all other things are nothing to us, why are we still troubled? why do we fear? The things for which we have been zealous are in no other man's power; and for the things that are in others' power we are not concerned. What difficulty have we now? *But direct me,* sayest thou. And why shall I direct thee? hath not God directed thee? hath He not given thee that which is thine own unhindered and unhampered, and hindered and hampered that which is not thine own? And what direction, what word of command didst thou receive from Him when thou camest thence? "Hold fast everything which is thine own—covet not that which is alien to thee. And faithfulness is thine, and reverence is thine: who, then, can rob thee of these things? who can hinder thee to use them, if not thyself? But thyself can do it, and how? When thou art zealous about things not thine own, and hast cast away the things that are." With such counsels and commands from Zeus, what wilt thou still from me? Am I greater than he? am I more worthy of thy faith? But if thou hold to these things, of what others hast thou need? *But perchance these are none of his commands?* Then bring forward the natural conceptions, bring the proofs of the philosophers, bring the things thou

hast often heard, bring the things that thyself hast spoken, bring what thou hast read, bring what thou hast pondered.

## CHAPTER V.

### THE PROMISE OF PHILOSOPHY.

1. OF things that exist, some are in our own power, some are not in our own power. Of things that are in our own power are our opinions, impulses, pursuits, avoidances, and, in brief, all that is of our own doing. Of things that are not in our own power are the body, possessions, reputation, authority, and, in brief, all that is not of our own doing. And the things that are in our own power are in their nature free, not liable to hindrance or embarrassment, while the things that are not in our own power are strengthless, servile, subject, alien.

2. Remember, then, if you hold things by their nature subject to be free, and things alien to be your proper concern, you will be hampered, you will lament, you will be troubled, you will blame Gods and men. But if you hold that only to be your own which is so, and the alien for what it is, alien, then none shall ever compel you, none shall hinder you, you will blame no one, accuse no one, you will not do the least thing unwillingly, none shall harm you, you shall have no foe, for you shall suffer no injury.

3. Aiming, then, at things so high, remember that it is no moderate passion wherewith you must attempt them, but some things you must utterly renounce, and put some, for the present, aside. For if, let us say, you aim also at this, to rule and to gather riches, then you are like, through aiming at the chief things also, to miss these lower ends; and shall most assuredly miss those others, through which alone freedom and happiness are won. Straightway, then, practise saying to every harsh appearance—*Thou art an Appearance and not at all the thing thou appearest to be.* Then examine it, and prove it by the rules you have, but first and above all by this, whether it concern something that is in our own power, or something that is not in our own power. And if the latter, then be the thought at hand: *It is nothing to Me.*

## CHAPTER VI.

### THE WAY OF PHILOSOPHY.

1. A CERTAIN Roman having entered with his son and listened to one lecture, "This," said Epictetus, "is the manner of teaching;" and he was silent. But when the other prayed him to continue, he spake as follows :—

Every art is wearisome, in the learning of it, to the untaught and unskilled. Yet things that are made by the arts immediately declare their use, and for what they were made, and in most of them is something attractive and pleasing. And thus when a shoemaker is learning his trade it is no pleasure to stand by and observe him, but the shoe is useful, and moreover not unpleasing to behold. And the learning of a carpenter's trade is very grievous to an untaught person who happens to be present, but the work done declares the need of the art. But far more is this seen in music, for if you are by where one is learning, it will appear the most painful of all instructions; but that which is produced by the musical art is sweet and delightful to hear, even to those who are untaught in it. And here we conceive the work of one who studies philosophy to be some such thing, that he must fit his desire to all events, so that nothing may come to pass against our will, nor may aught fail to come to pass that we wish for. Whence it results to those who so order it, that they never fail to obtain what they would, nor to avoid what they would not, living, as regards themselves, without pain, fear, or trouble; and as regards their fellows, observing all the relations, natural and acquired; as son or father, or brother or citizen, or husband or wife, or neighbour or fellow-traveller, or prince or subject. Such we conceive to be the work of one who pursues philosophy. And next we must inquire how this may come about.

2. We see, then, that the carpenter becomes a carpenter by learning something, and by learning something the pilot becomes a pilot. And here also is it

not on this wise? Is it enough that we merely wish to become good and wise, or must we not also learn something? We inquire, then, what we have to learn.

3. The philosphers say that, before all things, it is needful to learn that God is, and taketh thought for all things; and that nothing can be hid from him, neither deeds, nor even thoughts or wishes. Thereafter, of what nature the Gods are. For whatever they are found to be, he who would please and serve them must strive, with all his might, to be like unto them. If the Divine is faithful, so must he be faithful; if free, so must he be free; if beneficent, so must he be beneficent; if high-minded, so must he be high-minded; so that thus emulating God, he shall both do and speak the things that follow therefrom.[1]

4. Whence, then, shall we make a beginning? If you will consider this with me, I shall say, first, that you must attend to the sense of words.[2]

——"So I do not now understand them?"

You do not.

——"How, then, do I use them?".

As the unlettered use written words, or as cattle use appearances; for the use is one thing and understanding another. But if you think you understand, then take any word you will,[3] and let us try ourselves, whether we understand it. But it is hateful to be confuted, for a man now old,.and one who, perhaps, hath served his three campaigns? And I too know this. For you have come to me now as one who lacketh nothing. And what could you suppose to be lacking to you? Wealth have you, and children, and it may be a wife, and many servants; Cæsar knows you, you have won many friends in Rome, you give every man his due, you reward with good him that doeth good to you, and with evil him that doeth evil. What is still lacking to you? If, now, I shall show you that you lack the greatest and most necessary things for happiness, and that to this day you have cared for everything rather than for what behoved you; and if I crown all and say that you know not what God is nor what man is, nor Good nor Evil;—and what I say of other things is perhaps endurable, but if I say you know not your own self, how can you endure me, and bear the accusation, and abide here? Never—but straightway you will go away in anger. And yet what evil have I done you? Unless the mirror doth evil to the ill-favoured man, when it shows him to himself such as he is, and unless the physician is thought to affront the sick man when he may say to him: *Man, dost thou think thou ailest nothing? Thou hast a fever: fast to-day and drink water.* And none saith, *What an affront.* But if one shall say to a man: *Thy pursuits are inflamed, thine avoidances are mean, thy purposes are lawless, thy impulses accord not with nature, thine opinions are vain and lying*—straightway he goeth forth and saith, *He affronted me.*

5. We follow our business as in a great fair. Cattle and oxen are brought to be sold; and the greater part of the men come some to buy, some to sell; and few are they who come for the spectacle of the fair,—how it comes to pass, and wherefore, and

## THE WAY OF PHILOSOPHY.

who are they who have established it, and to what end. And so it is here, too, in this assembly of life. Some, indeed, like cattle, concern themselves with nothing but fodder; even such as those that care for possessions and lands and servants and offices, for these are nothing more than fodder. But few are they who come to the fair for love of the spectacle, what the world is and by whom it is governed. By no one? And how is it possible that a state or a house cannot endure, no not for the shortest time, without a governor and overseer, but this so great and fair fabric should be guided thus orderly by chance and accident? There is, then, one who governs. But what is his nature? and how doth he govern? and we, that were made by him, what are we, and for what are we? or have we at least some intercourse and link with him, or have we none? Thus it is that these few are moved, and thenceforth study this alone, to learn about the fair, and to depart. What then? they are mocked by the multitude. And in the fair, too, the observers are mocked by the traders; and had the cattle any reflection they would mock all those who cared for anything else than fodder.

## CHAPTER VII.

#### TO THE LEARNER.

1. REMEMBER that pursuit declares the aim of attaining the thing pursued, and avoidance that of not falling into the thing shunned; and he who fails in his pursuit is unfortunate, and it is misfortune to fall into what he would avoid. If now you shun only those things in your power which are contrary to Nature, you shall never fall into what you would avoid. But if you shun disease or death or poverty, you shall have misfortune.

2. Turn away, then, your avoidance from things not in our power, and set it upon things contrary to Nature which are in our power. And let pursuit for the present be utterly effaced; for if you are pursuing something that is not in our power, it must needs be that you miscarry, and of things that are, as many as you may rightly aim at, none are yet open to you. But use only desire and aversion, and that indeed lightly, and with reserve, and indifferently.

3. No great thing cometh suddenly into being, for not even a bunch of grapes can, or a fig. If you say to me now: *I desire a fig,* I answer that there is need of time: let it first of all flower, and then bring forth the fruit, and then ripen. When the fruit of a fig-tree is not perfected at once, and in a single hour, would you win the fruit of a man's mind thus quickly and easily? Even if I say to you, expect it not.

## TO THE LEARNER.

4. To fulfil the promise of a man's nature is itself no common thing. For what is a man? *A living creature*, say you; *mortal, and endowed with Reason.* And from what are we set apart by Reason? *From the wild beasts.* And what others? *From sheep and the like.* Look to it, then, that thou do nothing like a wild beast, for if thou do, the man in thee perisheth, thou hast not fulfilled his promise. Look to it, that thou do nothing like a sheep, or thus too the man hath perished. *What, then, can we do as sheep?* When we are gluttonous, sensual, reckless, filthy, thoughtless, to what are we then sunken?. To sheep. What have we lost? Our faculty of Reason. And when we are contentious, and hurtful, and angry and violent, to what are we sunken? To wild beasts. And for the rest some of us are great wild beasts, and some of us little and evil ones; whereby we may say, "Let me at least be eaten by a lion."[1] But through all these things the promise of the man's nature has been ruined.

5. For when is a complex proposition safe?[2] When it fulfils its promise. So that the validity of a complex proposition is when it is a complex of truths. And when is a disjunctive safe? When it fulfils its promise. And when are flutes, or a lyre, or a horse, or a dog? What marvel is it, then, if a man also is to be saved in the same way, and perish in the same way?

6. But each thing is increased and saved by the corresponding works—the carpenter by the practice of carpentry, the grammarian by the study

of grammar ; but if he use to write ungrammatically, it must needs be that his art shall be corrupted and destroyed. Thus, too, the works of reverence save the reverent man, and those of shamelessness destroy him. And works of faithfulness save the faithful man, and the contrary destroy him. And men of the contrary character are strengthened therein by contrary deeds ; the irreverent by irreverence, the faithless by faithlessness, the reviler by reviling, the angry by anger, the avaricious by unfair giving and taking.

7. Know, that not easily shall a conviction arise in a man unless he every day speak the same things and hear the same things, and at the same time apply them unto life.

8. Every great power is perilous to beginners. Thou must bear such things according to thy strength. *But I must live according to Nature?* That is not for a sick man.[3] Lead thy life as a sick man for a while, so that thou mayest hereafter live it as a whole man. Fast, drink water, abstain for a while from pursuit of every kind, in order that thou mayest pursue as Reason bids. And if as Reason bids, then when thou shalt have aught of good in thee, thy pursuit shall be well. *Nay, but we would live as sages and do good to men.* What good ? What will thou do ? Hast thou done good to thyself ? But thou would'st exhort them ? And hast thou exhorted thyself ?[4] Thou would'st do them good —then do not chatter to them, but show them in thyself what manner of men philosophy can make. In thy eating do good to those that eat with thee, in thy

drinking to those that drink, by yielding and giving place to all, and bearing with them. Thus do them good, and not by spitting thy bile upon them.

## CHAPTER VIII.

### THE CYNIC.[1]

1. ONE of his pupils, who seemed to be drawn towards the way of Cynism, inquired of Epictetus what manner of man the Cynic ought to be, and what was the natural conception of the thing. And Epictetus said: Let us look into it at leisure. But so much I have now to say to you, that whosoever shall without God attempt so great a matter stirreth up the wrath of God against him, and desireth only to behave himself unseemly before the people. For in no well-ordered house doth one come in and say to himself: *I should be the steward of the house*, else, when the lord of the house shall have observed it, and seeth him insolently giving orders, he will drag him forth and chastise him. So it is also in this great city of the universe, for here too there is a master of the house who ordereth each and all: 'Thou art the Sun; thy power is to travel round and to make the year and the seasons, and to increase and nourish fruits, and to stir the winds and still them, and temperately to warm the bodies of men. Go forth, run thy course,

and minister thus to the greatest things and to the least. Thou art a calf; when a lion shall appear, do what befits thee, or it shall be worse for thee. Thou art a bull; come forth and fight, for this is thy part and pride, and this thou canst. Thou art able to lead the army against Ilion; be Agamemnon. Thou canst fight in single combat with Hector; be Achilles. But if Thersites came forth and pretended to the authority, then either he would not gain it, or, gaining it, he would have been shamed before many witnesses.

2. And about this affair, do thou take thought upon it earnestly, for it is not such as it seemeth to thee. *I wear a rough cloak now, and I shall wear it then;*[2] *I sleep hard now, and I shall sleep so then. I will take to myself a wallet and staff, and I will begin to go about and beg, and to reprove everyone I meet with; and if I shall see one that plucks out his hairs, I will censure him, or one that hath his hair curled, or that goes in purple raiment.* If thou conceivest the matter on this wise, far be it from thee—go not near it, it is not for thee. But if thou conceivest of it as it is, and holdest thyself not unworthy of it, then behold to how great an enterprise thou art putting forth thine hand.

3. First, in things that concern thyself, thou must appear in nothing like unto what thou now doest. Thou must not accuse God nor man; thou must utterly give over pursuit, and avoid only those things that are in the power of thy will; anger is not meet for thee, nor resentment, nor envy, nor pity;[3] nor

must a girl appear to thee fair, nor must reputation, nor a flat cake.[4] For it must be understood that other men shelter themselves by walls and houses and by darkness when they do such things, and many means of concealment have they. One shutteth the door, placeth someone before the chamber; *if anyone should come, say, He is out, he is busy*. But in place of all these things it behoves the Cynic to shelter himself behind his own piety and reverence; but if he doth not, he shall be put to shame, naked under the sky. This is his house, this his door, this the guards of his chamber, this his darkness. For he must not seek to hide aught that he doeth, else he is gone, the Cynic hath perished, the man who lived under the open sky, the freeman. He hath begun to fear something from without, he hath begun to need concealment; nor can he find it when he would, for where shall he hide himself, and how? And if by chance this tutor, this public teacher, should be found in guilt, what things must he not suffer! And fearing these things, can he yet take heart with his whole soul to guide the rest of mankind? That can he never: it is impossible!

4. First, then, thou must purify thy ruling faculty, and this vocation of thine also, saying: Now it is my mind I must shape, as the carpenter shapes wood and the shoemaker leather; and the thing to be formed is a right use of appearances. But nothing to me is the body, and nothing to me the parts of it. *Death?* Let it come when it will, either death of the whole or of a part. *Flee it!* And whither? Can

any man cast me out of the universe? He cannot; but whithersoever I may go there will be the sun, and the moon, and there the stars, and visions, and omens, and communion with the Gods.⁵

5. And, furthermore, when he hath thus fashioned himself, he will not be content with these things, who is a Cynic indeed. But know that he is an herald from God to men, declaring to them the truth about good and evil things; that they have erred, and are seeking the reality of good and evil where it is not; and where it is, they do not consider; and he is a spy, like Diogenes, when he was led captive to Philip after the battle of Chæronea.⁶ For the Cynic is, in truth, a spy of the things that are friendly to men, and that are hostile; and having closely spied out all, he must come back and declare the truth. And he must neither be stricken with terror and report of enemies where none are; nor be in any otherwise confounded or troubled by the appearances.

6. He must then be able, if so it chance, to go up impassioned, as on the tragic stage, and speak that word of Socrates, "O men, whither are ye borne away? What do ye? Miserable as ye are! like blind men ye wander up and down. Ye have left the true road, and are going by a false; ye are seeking peace and happiness where they are not, and if another shall show you where they are, ye believe him not. Wherefore will ye seek it in outward things? *In the body?* It is not there—and if ye believe me not, lo, Myro! lo, Ophellius.⁷ *In possessions?* It is not there, and if ye believe me not, lo, Crœsus! lo, the wealthy of our own

day, how full of mourning is their life! *In authority?* It is not there, else should those be happy who have been twice or thrice consul; yet they are not. Whom shall we believe in this matter? You, who look but on these men from without, and are dazzled by the appearance, or the men themselves? And what say they? Hearken to them when they lament, when they groan, when by reason of those consulships, and their glory and renown, they hold their state the more full of misery and danger! *In royalty?* It is not there; else were Nero happy, and Sardanapalus; but not Agamemnon himself was happy, more splendid though he was than Nero or Sardanapalus; but while the rest are snoring what is he doing?

"He tore his rooted hair by handfuls out."—*Il.* x.

And what saith himself? "I am distraught," he saith, "and I am in anguish; my heart leaps forth from my bosom."—[*Il.* x.] Miserable man! which of thy concerns hath gone wrong with thee? Thy wealth? Nay. Thy body? Nay; but thou art rich in gold and bronze. What ails thee then? That part, whatever it be, with which we pursue, with which we avoid, with which we desire and dislike, thou hast neglected and corrupted. How hath it been neglected? He hath been ignorant of the true Good for which it was born, and of the Evil; and of what is his own, and what is alien to him. And when it goeth ill with something that is alien to him, he saith, "*Woe is me, for the Greeks are in peril.* O unhappy mind of thee! of all things alone neglected and untended. *They will be slain by the Trojans and die!* And if the Trojans slay them not, will they not still die? *Yea, but not all together.* What, then, doth it matter? for if it be an evil to die, it is alike evil to die together or to die one by one. Shall anything else happen to them than the parting of body and soul? *Nothing.* And when the Greeks have perished, is the door closed to thee? canst thou not also die? *I can.* Wherefore, then, dost thou lament: *Woe is me, a king, and bearing the sceptre of Zeus?* There is no unfortunate king, as there is no unfortunate God. What, then, art thou? In very truth a shepherd; for thou lamentest even as shepherds do when a wolf hath snatched away one of the sheep; and sheep are they whom thou dost rule. And why art thou come hither? Was thy faculty of pursuit in any peril, or of avoidance, or thy desire or aversion? *Nay,* he saith, *but my brother's wife was carried away.* Was it not a great gain to be rid of an adulterous wife? *Shall we be, then, despised of the Trojans?* Of the Trojans? Of what manner of men? of wise men or fools? If of wise men, why do ye make war with them? if of fools, why do ye heed them?[8]

7. *In what, then, is the good, seeing that in these things it is not? Tell us, thou, my lord missionary and spy!* It is there where ye deem it not, and where ye have no desire to seek it. For did ye desire, ye would have found it in yourselves, nor would ye wander to things without, nor pursue things alien, as if they were your own concerns. Turn to your own selves; understand the natural conceptions which ye

possess. What kind of thing do ye take the Good to be? Peace? happiness? freedom? Come, then, do ye not naturally conceive it as great, as precious, and that cannot be harmed? What kind of material, then, will ye take to shape peace and freedom withal—that which is enslaved or in that which is free? *That which is free.* Have ye the flesh enslaved or free? *We know not.* Know ye not that it is the slave of fever, of gout, of ophthalmia, of dysentery, of tyranny, and fire, and steel, and everything that is mightier than itself? *Yea, it is enslaved.* How, then, can aught that is of the body be free? and how can that be great or precious which by nature is dead, mere earth or mud?

8. What then? have ye nothing that is free? *It may be nothing.* And who can compel you to assent to an appearance that is false? *No man.* And who can compel you not to assent to an appearance that is true? *No man.* Here, then, ye see that there is in you something that is by nature free. But which of you, except he lay hold of some appearance of the profitable, or of the becoming, can either pursue or avoid, or desire or dislike, or adapt or intend anything? *No man.* In these things too, then, ye have something that is unhindered and free. This, miserable men, must ye perfect; this have a care to, in this seek for the Good.

9. *And how is it possible that one can live prosperously who hath nothing; a naked, homeless, hearthless, beggarly man, without servants, without a country?* Lo, God hath sent you a man to show you

in very deed that it is possible. "Behold me, that I have neither country, nor house, nor possessions, nor servants; I sleep on the ground; nor is a wife mine, nor children, nor domicile, but only earth and heaven, and a single cloak. And what is lacking to me? do ever I grieve? do I fear? am I not free? When did any of you see me fail of my pursuit, or meet with what I had avoided? When did I blame God or man? When did I accuse any man? When did any of you see me of a sullen countenance? How do I meet those whom ye fear and marvel at? Do I not treat them as my slaves? Who that seeth me, but thinketh he beholdeth his king and his lord?

10. So these are the accents of the Cynic, this his character, this his design. Not so—but it is his bag, and his staff, and his great jaws; and to devour all that is given to him, or store it up, or to reprove out of season everyone that he may meet, or to show off his shoulder.[9]

11. Dost thou see how thou art about to take in hand so great a matter? Take first a mirror, look upon thy shoulders, mark well thy loins and thighs. Thou art about to enter thy name for the Olympic games, O man; no cold and paltry contest. Nor canst thou then be merely overcome and then depart; but first thou must be shamed in the sight of all the world; and not alone of the Athenians or Lacedæmonians, or Nicopolitans. And then if thou hast too rashly entered upon the contest, thou must be thrashed, and before being thrashed must suffer thirst and scorching heat, and swallow much dust.

12. Consider more closely, know thyself, question thy genius,[10] attempt nothing without God; who, if he counsel thee, be sure that he wills thee either to be great or to be greatly plagued. For this very agreeable circumstance is linked with the calling of a Cynic; he must be flogged like an ass, and, being flogged, must love those who flog him, as though he were the father or brother of all mankind. Not so, but if one shall flog thee, stand in the midst and shriek out, *O Cæsar, what things do I suffer in the Emperor's peace! Let us take him before the pro-consul.* But what is Cæsar to the Cynic? or what is a pro-consul? or what is any other than He that hath sent him hither, and whom he serveth, which is Zeus? Doth he call upon any other than God? Is he not persuaded, whatsoever things he may suffer, that he is being trained and exercised by God? Hercules, when he was exercised by Eurystheus, never deemed himself wretched; but fulfilled courageously all that was laid upon him. But he who shall cry out and bear it hard when he is being trained and exercised by Zeus, is he worthy to bear the sceptre of Diogenes? Hear what Diogenes saith, when ill of a fever, to the bystanders: *Base souls, will ye not remain? To see the overthrow and combat of athletes, how great a way ye journey to Olympia; and have ye no will to see a combat between a fever and a man?* And will such an one presently accuse God who hath sent him, as having used him ill —he who was glorying in his lot, and held himself worthy to be a spectacle to the bystanders? For of what shall he accuse Him: that his life is seemly, that

he manifests God's will, that he showeth forth his virtue more brightly? Come, then; and what saith he about death, about pain? How did he compare his own happiness with that of the Great King? nay, he thought rather that there was no comparison. For where there are confusions, and griefs, and fears, and unattained pursuits, and avoidance in vain, and envy and rivalry, can the way to happiness lie there? But where rotten opinions are there must of necessity be all these things.

13. And the young man having asked whether one that hath fallen ill shall obey, if a friend desire that he will go home with him and be tended: Where, he said, will you show me the friend of a Cynic? For he himself must be even such another, so as to be worthy to be reckoned his friend. A sharer in the sceptre and the royalty must he be, and a worthy servant, if he will be worthy of his friendship, as Diogenes was of Antisthenes and Crates of Diogenes. Or seems it so to thee that whosoever shall come to him and bid him hail is his friend? and that he will think him worthy that a Cynic shall go to his house? Thus, if it please thee to be a Cynic, bethink thee rather of such a thing as this, and cast about for a dainty dungheap whereon to have thy fever; and see that it look away from the north, so that thou be not chilled. But thou seemest to me to wish to retreat into somebody's house and spend thy time there, and be fed. What hast thou to do with undertaking so great a matter?

14. *But marriage,* said he, *and the begetting of*

## THE CYNIC.

children,—are these to be received by the Cynic among his chief purposes?

Give me, said Epictetus, a city of wise men, and perhaps no one will easily come to the Cynic way: for whose sake should he embrace it? However, if we do suppose such a thing, there is nothing to hinder his marrying and begetting children; for his wife will be even such another, and his father-in-law such another, and thus will his children be brought up. But things being as they now are, as it were in order of battle, must not the Cynic be given wholly and undistracted to the service of God, being able to go about among men, and not bound to private duties, nor entangled in ties which, if he transgress, he can no longer preserve the aspect of honesty and goodness; and if he obey them, he hath lost that of the missionary, the spy, the herald of the Gods? For see! he must needs observe a certain conduct towards his father-in-law, and he hath somewhat to render also to the rest of his wife's kin and to his wife herself. And for the rest, he is shut off from Cynism by the care for sickness, or means of livelihood. For one thing alone, he must have a vessel for warming water for his little child, where he may wash it in the bath; and wool for his wife when she has been delivered, and oil, and a couch, and a drinking cup—already a number of utensils —and other affairs and distractions. Where shall I thenceforth find that king, whose whole business is the common weal?

"Warden of men, and with so many cares."—(*Il.* ii., 25),

539

on whom it lies to oversee all men, the married, and parents, and who useth his wife well, and who ill, and who wrangles, and what household is well-ordered, and what not; going about as a physician, and feeling pulses—"thou hast a fever, thou a headache, thou the gout; do thou fast, do thou eat, do thou avoid the bath, thou needest the knife, thou the cautery?" Where is the place for leisure to one who is bound to private duties? Must he not provide raiment for his children? yea, and send them to the schoolmaster with their tablets and writing instruments? and have a bed ready for them, since a man cannot be a Cynic from the womb? Else were it better to cast them away at once than kill them in this way. See, now, to what we have brought our Cynic—how we have taken away his kingship from him! *True, but Crates married.* Thou speakest of a circumstance that arose from love, and adducest a wife who was another Crates.[11] But our inquiry is concerning common marriages, and how men may be undistracted; and thus inquiring, we do not find it, in this condition of the world, a purpose of chief concern for a Cynic.

15. *How, then,* said he, *shall he still be preserving the community?* God help thee! Whether do they best serve mankind who fill their own place by bringing into the world two or three screaming children, or those who, as far they may, oversee all men, what they do, how they live, wherewith they concern themselves, and what duties they neglect? And were the Thebans more benefited by as many as

left their little children behind, or by Epaminondas, who died childless? And did Priam, who begat fifty good-for-nothing sons, or Danaus, or Æolus,[12] better serve the community than Homer?. Shall, then, the command of an army or the writing of poems withdraw a man from marriage and fatherhood, and he shall not be thought to have gained nothing for his childlessness, but the kingship of a Cynic shall be not worth what it costs? It may be we do not perceive his greatness, nor do we worthily conceive of the character of Diogenes; but we turn away our eyes to the present Cynics, "watch-dogs of the dining-room,"[13] who in nothing resemble those others, save perchance in breaking wind; but in no other thing. For else these things would not have moved us, nor should we have marvelled if a Cynic will not marry nor beget children. Man! he hath begotten all mankind, he hath all men for his sons, all women for his daughters; so doth he visit all and care for all. Thinkest thou that he is a mere meddler and busybody in rebuking those whom he meets? As a father he doth it, as a brother, and as servant of the Universal Father, which is God.

16. If it please thee, ask of me also whether he shall have to do with affairs of public polity? Fool! dost thou seek a greater polity than that in whose affairs he is already concerned? Will it be greater if he come forward among the Athenians to say something about ways or means—he, whose part it is to discourse with all men, Athenians, Corinthians, Romans alike, not concerning means or ways, nor concerning

peace or war, but about happiness and unhappiness, about good-fortune and ill-fortune, about slavery and freedom? And of a man that hath his part in so great a polity will you ask me if he shall attend to public affairs? Ask me also if he shall be a ruler; and again I shall say, Thou fool, what rule can be greater than his?

17. And to such a man there is need also of a certain kind of body. For if he shall appear consumptive, meagre, and pale, his witness hath not the same emphasis. Not only by showing forth the things of the spirit must he convince foolish men that it is possible, without the things that are admired of them, to be good and wise, but also in his body must he show that plain and simple and open-air living are not mischievous even to the body: " Behold, even of this I am a witness, I and my body." So Diogenes was wont to do, for he went about radiant with health, and with his very body he turned many to good. But a Cynic that men pity seems to be a beggar—all men turn away from him, all stumble at him. For he must not appear squalid; so that neither in this respect shall he scare men away; but his very austerity should be cleanly and pleasing.

18. Much grace of body, then, must belong to the Cynic, and also quickness of mind, else he is a mere clot of slime and nothing else; for he must be ready and apt to meet all that may befall him. Thus when one said to Diogenes: *Thou art that Diogenes who thinkest there are no Gods,* he replied, *And how may that be, seeing I hold thee hateful to the Gods?* And again,

when Alexander stood beside him, as he was lying asleep, and said:

"Not all night must a man of counsel sleep,"

he answered, ere he was yet awake:

"Warden of men, and with so many cares."[14]

19. But before all things must his ruling faculty be purer than the sun, else he must needs be a gambler and cheater, who, being himself entangled in some iniquity, will reprove others. For, see how the matter stands: to these kings and tyrants, their spearmen and their arms give the office of reproving men, and the power to punish transgressors, yea, though they themselves be evil; but to the Cynic, instead of arms and spearmen, his conscience giveth this power. When he knows that he has watched and laboured for men, and lain down to sleep in purity, and sleep hath left him yet purer; and that his thoughts have been the thoughts of one dear to the Gods, of a servant, and a sharer in the rule of Zeus; and he hath had ever at hand that

"Lead me, O Zeus, and thou Destiny,[15]

and,

"If thus it be pleasing to the Gods, so may it be"—

wherefore, then, shall he not take heart to speak boldly to his brothers, to his children, in a word, to all his kin? For this reason, he that in this state is no meddler or busybody, for when he overlooks human affairs he meddles not with foreign matters, but with his own affairs. Else, name the general a busybody when he overlooks his soldiers, and reviews them, and watches them, and punishes the disorderly. But if you have a flat cake under your cloak while you reprove others, I say, get hence rather into a corner, and eat what thou hast stolen—what are other men's concerns to thee? For what art thou—the bull of the herd? or the queen bee? Show me the tokens of thy supremacy, such as nature hath given her. But if thou art a drone claiming sovereignty over the bees, thinkest thou not that thy fellow-citizens will overthrow thee, as bees do the drones?

20. And truly the Cynic must be so long-suffering as that he shall seem to the multitude insensate and a stone. Him doth none revile, nor smite, nor insult; but his body hath he given to any man to use at will. For he remembers that the worse must needs be vanquished by the better, wheresoever it is the worse; and the body is worse than the multitude—the weaker than the stronger. Never, then, doth he go down to any contest where it is possible for him to be vanquished, but he yields up all that is not his own, and contends for nothing that is subject to others. But where there is question of the will and the use of appearances, then you shall see how many eyes he hath, so that you may say that compared with him Argus was blind. Is his assent ever hasty; or his desire idle; or his pursuit in vain; or his avoidance unsuccessful; or his aim unfulfilled? doth he ever blame, or cringe, or envy? This is his great study and his design; but as regards

## THE CYNIC.

all other things, he lies on his back and snores, for all is peace. There is no thief of his will, nor tyrant; but of his body? yea; and of his chattels? yea, and also of his authority and his honours. What, then, are these things to him? So when one may seek to make him afraid on account of them,—*Go hence*, he saith to him, *and find out little children; it is to these that masks are dreadful, but I know they are made of clay, and that inside them there is nothing.*

21. On such a matter art thou now meditating. Therefore, if it please thee, in God's name delay it yet awhile, and see first what ability thou hast for it. For mark what Hector speaks to Andromache: *Go*, he saith, *rather into the house and weave*—

> "For war's the care
> Of every man, and more than all of me."
> —*Il.* vi. 490.

Thus he knew where lay his own ability and her incapacity.

END OF BOOK I.

# BOOK II.

## CHAPTER I.

ON GENUINE AND BORROWED BELIEFS.

1. THE master-argument seems to start from propositions such as these:[1] There being a mutual contradiction among these three propositions—(1) "Every past event is necessarily true," and (2) "An impossibility cannot follow a possibility," and (3) "Things are possible which neither are nor will be true," Diodorus, perceiving this contradiction, made use of the force of the first two in order to prove that nothing is possible which neither is nor will be true. And, again, one will hold these two, (3) that a thing is possible which neither is nor will be true, and (2) that an impossibility cannot follow from a possibility; but by no means that every past thing is necessarily true, and thus those of the school of Cleanthes appear to think, whom Antipater strongly defended. But some hold the other two, (3) that a thing is possible that neither is nor will be true, and (1) that every past event is necessarily true; but maintain that an impossibility may follow from a possibility. But all three it is

impossible to hold at once, because of their mutual contradiction.

2. Now, if anyone inquire of me, *And which of these dost thou hold?* I shall answer him that I do not know, but I have received this account, that Diodorus holds certain of them, and I think the followers of Panthoides and Cleanthes certain others, and those of Chrysippus yet others. *And thyself?* Nay, it is no affair of mine to try my own thoughts, and to compare and estimate statements, and to form some opinion of my own upon the matter.² And thus I differ no whit from the grammarians. Who was Hector's father? *Priam.* And his brothers? *Alexander and Deiphobus.* And their mother, who was she? *Hecuba. That is the account I have received.* From whom? *From Homer; and I think Hellanicus has written of them, and maybe others too.* And I; what better have I to say about the master argument? But if I am a vain man, and especially at a banquet, I shall amaze all the company by recounting those who have written on it;—for Chrysippus wrote on it wonderfully in his first book " On Possibilities ;" and Cleanthes wrote a separate treatise on it, and so did Archedemus. And Antipater wrote too, not only in his book, " On Possibilities," but also separately in those on the master argument. Have you not read the work? No! Then read it. And what good will it do him to read it? He will become yet more of a babbler and a nuisance than he is now, for what else hath the reading of it done for you? What opinion have you formed for

yourself on the matter? Nay, but you will tell us all about Helen, and Priam, and the island of Calypso, that never existed, nor ever will.

3. And in Homer, indeed, it is no great matter if you have simply mastered the account, and formed no opinion of your own. But in ethics this is even much more often the case than in other matters. Tell me concerning good and evil things! Listen to him, then, with his—

"Me to Ciconia brought the wind from Troy."[3]—*Od.* ix. 39.

*Of things some are good, some evil, and some indifferent. Now the good things are the virtues, and those that have the nature of virtue, and the evil things the vices, and those that have the nature of vice; and the indifferent things are between these, as wealth, health, life, death, pleasure, affliction.* And how do you know this? Because Hellanicus affirms it in his history of the Egyptians; for as well say this as that Diogenes has it in his Ethics, or Chrysippus, or Cleanthes. But have you tested any of their sayings, and formed an opinion for yourself? Show me how you are wont to bear a storm at sea. Do you remember the difference between good and evil when the sail clatters, and some vexatious man comes to you as you are shrieking, and says—

——"Tell me, by the gods, what you were lately saying, Is it any vice to be shipwrecked? Hath it anything of the nature of vice?"

Would you not lay hold of a stick and shake it in his face: *Let us alone, man; we are perishing, and you come to mock us!* And do you remember the difference if you are accused of something and Cæsar sends for you? If one should come to you when you enter, pale and trembling, and should say, "Why do you tremble, man? what is your business concerned with? Doth Cæsar there within dispense virtue and vice to those who go in to him? *Why, you will say; must you too mock me in my calamities?*

——" Nevertheless, tell me, O Philosopher, why you tremble—is it not merely death that you are in danger of, or imprisonment, or bodily suffering, or exile, or disgrace? What else? Is it any vice? or anything of the nature of vice?"

And you will reply somewhat to this effect: *Let me alone, man; my own evils are enough for me.*

And truly you say well, for your own evils are enough for you; which are meanness, cowardice, and your false pretences when you sat in the school of philosophy. Why did you deck yourself in others' glory? Why did you call yourself a Stoic?

4. Watch yourselves thus in the things that ye do, and ye shall see of what school ye are. And the most of you will be found Epicureans, but some few Peripatetics,⁴ and those but slack. For where is the proof that ye hold virtue equal to all other things, or indeed superior? Show me a Stoic, if ye have one. Where or how can ye? But persons that repeat the phrases of Stoicism, of these ye can show us any number. And do they repeat those of the Epicureans any worse? and are they not equally accurate in the Peripatetic? Who is, then, a Stoic? As we say that

a statue is Pheidian which is wrought according to the art of Pheidias, show me a man that is wrought according to the opinions he utters! Show me one that is sick and yet prosperous, in peril and prosperous, dying and prosperous, in exile and prosperous, in evil repute and prosperous Show him to me! by the Gods! fain would I see a Stoic! And have ye none that is fully wrought out; then show me at least one that is in hand to be wrought—one that even leaneth towards these things. Do me this favour— grudge not an old man a sight that I have never seen yet. Think ye that I would have you show me the Zeus of Pheidias or the Athene—a work all ivory and gold? Nay; but let one show me a man's soul that longs to be like-minded with God, and to blame neither Gods nor men, and not to fail in any effort or avoidance, and not to be wrathful nor envious, nor jealous, but—for why should I make rounds to say it? —that desires to become a God from a man, and in this body of ours, this corpse, is mindful of his fellowship with Zeus. Show me that man. But ye cannot! Why, then, will ye mock yourselves and cheat others? Why wrap yourselves in others' garb, and go about, like thieves that steal clothes from the bath, with names and things that in nowise belong to you?

5. And now I am your teacher and ye are being taught by me. And I have this aim—to perfect you, that ye be unhindered, uncompelled, unembarrassed, free, prosperous, happy, looking unto God alone in all things great and small. And ye are here to learn these things, and to do them. And wherefore do ye

not finish the work, if ye have indeed such an aim as behoves you, and if I, besides the aim, have such ability as behoves me? What is here lacking? When I see a carpenter, and the wood lying beside him, I look for some work. And now, here is the carpenter, here is the wood—what is yet lacking? Is the thing such as cannot be taught? It can. Is it, then, not in our power? Yea, this alone of all things is. Wealth is not in our power, nor health, nor repute, nor any other thing, save only the right use of appearances. This alone is by nature unhindered; this alone is unembarrassed. Wherefore, then, will ye not make an end? Tell me the reason. For either the fault lies in me, or in you, or in the nature of the thing. But the thing itself is possible, and indeed the only thing that is in our power. It remains that I am to blame, or else ye are; or, to speak more truly, both of us. What will ye, then? Let us at length begin to entertain such a purpose among us, and let the past be past. Only let us make a beginning: trust in me, and ye shall see.

## CHAPTER II.

### THE GAME OF LIFE.

1. THIS above all is the task of Nature—to bind and harmonise together the force of the appearances of the Right and of the Useful.

2. Things are indifferent, but the uses of them are

not indifferent. How, then, shall one preserve at once both a steadfast and tranquil mind, and also carefulness of things, that he be not heedless or slovenly? If he take example of dice players. The numbers are indifferent, the dice are indifferent. How can I tell what may be thrown up? But carefully and skilfully to make use of what is thrown, that is where my proper business begins. And this is the great task of life also, to discern things and divide them, and say, "Outward things are not in my power; to will is in my power. Where shall I seek the Good, and where the Evil? Within me—in all that is my own." But of all that is alien to thee call nothing good nor evil nor profitable nor hurtful, nor any such term as these.

3. What then? should we be careless of such things? In no wise. For this, again, is a vice in the Will, and thus contrary to Nature. But be at once careful, because the use of things is not indifferent, and steadfast and tranquil because the things themselves are. For where there is aught that concerns me, there none can hinder or compel me; and in those things where I am hindered or compelled the attainment is not in my power, and is neither good nor evil; but my use of the event is either evil or good, and this is in my power. And hard it is, indeed, to mingle and reconcile together the carefulness of one whom outward things affect, with the steadfastness of him who regards them not. But impossible it is not; and if it is, it is impossible to be happy.

4. Give me one man that cares how he shall do

anything—that thinks not of the gaining of the thing, but thinks of his own energy.

5. Chrysippus, therefore, said well—"As long as future things are hidden from me, I hold always by whatever state is the most favourable for gaining the things that are according to Nature; for God himself gave it to me to make such choice. But if I knew that it were now ordained for me to be sick, I would even move to it of myself. For the foot, too, if it had intelligence, would move of itself to be mired.

6. For to what end, think you, are ears of corn produced? Is it not that they may become dry and parched? And the reason they are parched, is it not that they may be reaped? for it is not to exist for themselves alone that they come into the world. If, then, they had perception, would it be proper for them to pray that they should never be reaped? since never to be reaped is for ears of corn a curse. So understand that for men it is a curse not to die, just as not to be ripened and not to be reaped. But we, since we are both the things to be reaped and are also conscious that we shall be reaped, have indignation thereat. For we know not what we are, nor have we studied what concerns humanity, as those that have the care of horses study what concerns them. But Chrysantas, when just about to smite the enemy, forbore on hearing the trumpet sounding his recall; so much better did it seem to him to obey the commander's order than to do his own will. But of us not one will follow with docility the summons even of necessity, but weeping and groaning the things that

we suffer, we suffer, calling them our doom.[1] What doom, man? If by doom you mean that which is doomed to happen to us, then we are doomed in all things. But if only our afflictions are to be called doom, then what affliction is it that that which has come into being should perish? But we perish by the sword, or the wheel, or the sea, or the tile of a roof, or a tyrant. What matters it by what road thou goest down into Hades? they are all equal. But if thou wilt hear the truth, the way the tyrant sends thee is the shortest. Never did any tyrant cut a man's throat in six months, but a fever will often be a year killing him. All these things are but noise, and a clatter of empty names.

7. But let us do as in setting out on a voyage. What is it possible for me to do? This—to choose the captain, crew, the day, the opportunity. Then a tempest has burst upon us; but what doth it concern me? I have left nothing undone that was mine to do; the problem is now another's, to wit, the captain's. But now the ship is sinking! and what have I to do? I do only what I am able—drown without terror and screaming and accusing of God, but knowing that that which has come into being must also perish. For I am no Immortal, but a man, a part of the sum of things as an hour is of the day. Like the hour I must arrive, and, like the hour, pass away. What, then, can it matter to me how I pass away—whether by drowning or by a fever? for pass I must, even by some such thing. Now, this is what you shall see done by skilful ball-players. None careth for the ball as it

were a thing good or bad; but only about throwing it and catching it. In this, then, there is rule, in this art, quickness, judgment; so that I may fail of catching the ball, even if I spread out my lap, and another, if I throw it, may catch it. But if I am anxious and nervous as I catch and throw, what kind of play is this? how shall one be steady? how shall he observe the order of the game? One will call "Throw," "Do not throw," and another, "You have thrown once." But this is strife and not play.

8. Thus Socrates knew how to play ball. How? When he jested in the court of justice. "Tell me, Anytus," he said, "how say you that I believe there is no God? The Dæmons, who are they, think you? Are they not sons of God, or a mixed nature between Gods and men?" And when this was admitted—"Who, do you think, can hold that mules exist, but not asses?"[2] And thus he played with the ball. And what was the ball that was there thrown about among them? Life, chains, exile, a draught of poison, to be torn from a wife, to leave children orphans. These were the things among them that they played withal; yet none the less did he play, and flung the ball with proper grace and measure. And so should we do also, having the carefulness of the most zealous players, and yet indifference, as were it merely about a ball.

## CHAPTER III.

#### THINGS ARE WHAT THEY ARE.

1. EACH thing that allures the mind, or offers an advantage, or is loved by you, remember to speak of it as it is, from the smallest things upward. If you love an earthen jar, then think, *I love an earthen jar*, for so shall you not be troubled when it breaks. And when you kiss your little child, or wife, think, *I kiss a mortal;* and so shall you not be troubled when they die.

2. When you are about to take in hand some action, bethink you what it is that you are about to do. If you go to the bath, represent to yourself all that takes place there—the squirting of water, the slapping, the scolding, the pilfering; and then shall you take the matter in hand more safely, saying straightway: *I desire to be bathed, and maintain my purpose according to Nature.* And even so with each and every action. For thus, if aught should occur to cross you in your bathing, this thought shall be straightway at hand: *But not this alone did I desire; but also to maintain my purpose according to Nature. And I shall not maintain it if I have indignation at what happens here.*

3. The first difference between the vulgar man[1] and the philosopher: The one saith, *Woe is me for my child, my brother, woe for my father;* but the other, if ever he shall be compelled to say, *Woe is me,* checks

himself and saith, *for myself.* For nothing that the Will willeth not can hinder or hurt the Will, but itself only can hurt itself. If then, indeed, we too incline to this, that when we are afflicted we accuse ourselves, and recollect that nothing else than Opinion can cause us any trouble or unsettlement, I swear by all the Gods we have advanced! But as it is, we have from the beginning travelled a different road. While we are still children, if haply we stumbled as we were gaping about, the nurse did not chide us, but beat the stone. For what had the stone done? Ought it to have moved out of the way, for your child's folly? Again, if we find nothing to eat after coming from the bath, never doth the tutor check our desire, but he beats the cook. Man, we did not set thee to be a tutor of the cook, but of our child—him shall you train, him improve. And thus, even when full-grown, we appear as children. For a child in music is he who hath not learned music, and in letters, one who hath not learned letters, and in life, one undisciplined in philosophy.

4. It is not things, but the opinions about the things, that trouble mankind. Thus Death is nothing terrible; if it were so, it would have appeared so to Socrates. But the opinion we have about Death, that it is terrible, *that* it is wherein the terror lieth. When, therefore, we are hindered or troubled or grieved, never let us blame any other than ourselves; that is to say, our opinions. A man undisciplined in philosophy blames others in matters in which he fares ill; one who begins to be disciplined blames himself, one who is disciplined, neither others nor himself.

5. Be not elated in mind at any superiority that is not of yourself. If your horse were elated and should say, *I am beautiful*, that would be tolerable. But when you are elated and say, *I have a beautiful horse*, know that it is at an excellence in your horse that you are elated. What, then, is your own? This —to make use of the appearances. So that when you deal according to Nature in the use of appearances, then shall you be elated, for you will then be elated at an excellence that is your own.

## CHAPTER IV.

### THREE STEPS TO PERFECTION.

1. THERE are three divisions of Philosophy wherein a man must exercise himself who would be wise and good.[1]

The first concerns his pursuit and avoidance, so that he may not fail of aught that he would attain, nor fall into aught that he would avoid.

The second concerns his desires and aversions, and, generally, all that it becomes a man to be, so that he bear himself orderly and prudently and not heedlessly.

The third is that which concerns security from delusion and hasty apprehension, and, generally, the assenting to appearances.

Of these the chief and most urgent is that which

## THREE STEPS TO PERFECTION. 53

hath to do with the passions,[2] for the passions arise in no other way than by our failing in endeavour to attain or to avoid something. This it is which brings in troubles and tumults and ill-luck and misfortune, that is the cause of griefs and lamentations and envies, that makes envious and jealous men; by which things we become unable even to hear the doctrines of reason.

The second concerns that which is becoming to a man; for I must not be passionless,[3] like a statue, but maintain all relations natural and acquired, as a religious being, as a son, as a brother, as a father, as a citizen.

The third is that which concerns men as soon as they are making advance in philosophy, which provides for the security of the two others; so that not even in dreams may any appearance that approacheth us pass untested, nor in wine, nor in ill-humours. This, a man may say, is beyond us. But the philosophers of this day, passing by the first and second parts of philosophy, occupy themselves in the third, cavilling, and arguing by questions, and constructing hypotheses and fallacies. For, they say, when dealing with these subjects a man must guard himself from delusion. Who must? The wise and good man.

2. And this security is all you lack, then; the rest you have wrought out already? You are not to be imposed upon by money? and if you see a fair girl you can hold out against the appearance? and if your neighbour inherits a legacy you are not envious?

there is now, in short, nothing lacking to you except to confirm what you have? Wretch! these very things. dost thou hear in fear and anxiety lest some one may despise thee, and inquiring what men say about thee. And if someone come and tell you that when it was discussed who was the best of the philosophers, one present said, *Such a one is the greatest philosopher,* your little soul will grow up from a finger's breadth to two cubits. And if another who was present said, *Nothing of the kind; it is not worth while to listen to him; for what does he know? he has made a beginning in philosophy and no more,* you are amazed, you grow pale, and straightway you cry out, *I will show him who I am, that I am a great philosopher.*

Out of these very things it is seen what you are; why do you desire to show it by any others?

---

## CHAPTER V.

### THAT A MAN MAY BE BOTH BOLD AND FEARFUL.

1. To some it may perchance seem a paradox, this axiom of the philosophers; yet let us make the best inquiry we can if it be true that it is possible to do all things at once with fearfulness and with boldness. For fearfulness seemeth in a manner contrary to boldness, and contraries can never coexist. But that which to many seemeth a paradox in this matter

seems to me to stand somehow thus: If we affirmed that both fearfulness and boldness could be used in the very same things, they would justly accuse us that we were reconciling what is irreconcilable. But now, what is there so strange in this saying? For if it is sound, what hath been so often both affirmed and demonstrated, that the essence of the Good is in the use of appearances, and even so of the Evil, and things uncontrollable by the Will have the nature neither of good nor of evil, what paradox do the philosophers affirm if they say that in things uncontrollable by the Will, then be boldness thy part, and in things subject to the Will, fearfulness. For if Evil lie in an evil Will, then in these things alone is it right to use fearfulness. And if things uncontrollable by the Will, and that are not in our power, are nothing to us, then in these things we should use boldness. And thus shall we be at one time both fearful and bold—yea, and bold even through our fearfulness. For through being fearful in things that are veritably evil it comes that we shall be bold in those that are not so.

2. But we, on the contrary, fall victims as deer do. When these are terrified and fly from the scares, whither do they turn and to what do they retreat as a refuge? To the nets: and thus they perish, confusing things to fear and things to be bold about. And thus do we also. Where do we employ fear? In things beyond our Will. And wherein do we act boldly, as were there nothing to dread? In things subject to the Will. To be beguiled, then, or to be

rash, or to do some shameless act, or with base greed to pursue some object—these things concern us no whit if we may only hit the mark in things beyond the Will. But where death is, or exile, or suffering, or evil repute, there we run away, there we are scared. Therefore, as it were to be looked for in those who are astray in the things of greatest moment, we work out our natural boldness into swaggering, abandonment, rashness, shamelessness; and our natural fearfulness and shamefastness into cowardice and meanness, full of terror and trouble. For if one should transfer his fearfulness to the realm of the Will, and the works thereof, straightway, together with the intention of fearing to do wrong he shall have it in his power to avoid doing it; but if he use it in things out of our own power and beyond the Will, then striving to avoid things that are in others' power he shall of necessity be terrified and unsettled and troubled. For death is not fearful, nor pain, but the fear of pain or death. And thus we praise him[1] who said:

"Fear not to die, but fear a coward's death."

3. It is right, then, that we should turn our boldness against death, and our fearfulness against the fear of death. But now we do the contrary: death we flee from, but as to the state of our opinion about death we are negligent, heedless, indifferent. These things Socrates did well to call bugbears. For as to children, through their inexperience, ugly masks appear terrible and fearful; so we are

somewhat in the same way moved towards the affairs of life, for no other cause than as children are affected by these bugbears. For what is a child? Ignorance. What is a child? That which has never learned. For when he knows these things he is nowise inferior to us. What is death? A bugbear. Turn it round; examine it: see, it does not bite. Now or later that which is body must be parted from that which is spirit, as formerly it was parted. Why, then, hast thou indignation if it be now? for if it be not now, it will be later. And wherefore? That the cycle of the world may be fulfilled; for it hath need of a present and of a future and of a past. What is pain? A bugbear. Turn it about and examine it. This poor body is moved harshly, then again softly. If thou hast no advantage thereof, the door is open;[2] if thou hast, then bear it. For in all events it is right that the door should stand open, and so have we no distress.

4. Shall I, then, exist no longer? Nay, thou shalt exist, but as something else, whereof the universe hath now need.[3] For neither didst thou choose thine own time to come into existence, but when the universe had need of thee.

5. What, then, is the fruit of these opinions? That which ought to be the fairest and comeliest to those who have been truly taught,—tranquillity, courage, and freedom. For concerning these things, the multitude are not to be believed which say that those only should be taught who are freemen, but the philosophers rather, which say that those only are

free who have been taught. How is this? It is thus—Is freedom anything else than the power to live as we choose? *Nothing else.* Do ye choose, then, to live in sin? *We do not choose it.* None, therefore, that fears or grieves or is anxious is free; but whosoever is released from griefs and fears and anxieties is by that very thing released from slavery. How, then, shall we still believe you, most excellent legislators, when ye say, "We permit none to be taught, save freemen?"⁴ for the philosophers say, "We permit none to be free save those who have been taught"— that is, God permits it not. *So, when a man turns round his slave before the Prætor,⁵ has he done nothing?* He has done something. *And what?* He has turned round his slave before the Prætor. *Nothing else at all?* Yea, this too—he must pay for him the tax of the twentieth. *What then? has the man thus treated not gained his freedom?* No more than he has gained tranquillity of mind. For thou, who art able to emancipate others, hast thou no master? is money not thy master, or lust, or a tyrant, or some friend of a tyrant? Why, then, dost thou tremble when thou art to meet with some affliction in this kind? And therefore I say oftentimes, be these things your study, be these things ever at your hand, wherein ye should be bold and wherein fearful ; bold in things beyond the Will, fearful in things subject to the Will.

## CHAPTER VI.[1]

### THE WISE MAN'S FEAR AND THE FOOL'S.

1. THE appearances by which the mind of man is smitten with the first aspect of a thing as it approaches the soul, are not matters of the will, nor can we control them; but by a certain force of their own the objects which we have to comprehend are borne in upon us. But that ratification of them, which we name assent, whereby the appearances are comprehended and judged, these are voluntary, and are done by human choice. Wherefore at a sound from the heavens, or from the downfall of something, or some signal of danger, or anything else of this kind, it must needs be that the soul of the philosopher too shall be somewhat moved, and he shall shrink and grow pale; not through any opinion of evil that he has formed, but through certain rapid and unconsidered motions that forestal the office of the mind and reason. Soon, however, that philosopher doth not approve the appearances to be truly objects of terror to his soul,— that is to say, he assents not to them nor ratifies them; but he rejects them, and casts them out; nor doth there seem to be in them anything that he should fear. But in this, say the philosophers, doth the wise man differ from the fool,—that the fool thinks the appearances to be in truth even so harsh and rough as they seemed at their first shock upon the soul; and taking them, as at first, to be rightly dreaded, he thus ratifies

and approves them by his assent. The philosopher, however, though for a short time his colour and countenance have been changed, doth not then assent, but he retains in its steadfastness and vigour the opinion he ever had of these appearances, that they are in no wise to be feared, but affright only by a false show and empty threat.

2. Such as is a dish of water, such is the soul; such as is the ray of light that falleth on the same, such are the appearances. When the water is moved, then the ray seemeth also to be moved; but it is not moved. And thus when a man's mind is darkened and dizzy, it is not doctrines and virtues that are confounded, but the spirit on which they are impressed. And if that is restored, so are they.[2]

## CHAPTER VII.

### APPEARANCES FALSE AND TRUE.

1. APPEARANCES exist for us in four ways. Either things appear even as they are; or having no existence, neither do they appear to have it; or they exist, and appear not; or they exist not, and yet appear. So, in all these cases, to hit the mark is the work of him who hath been taught in philosophy.

2. But whatever it be that afflicts us, it is to that thing that the remedy is to be applied. If it is the

sophisms of the Pyrrhonists and Academics[1] that afflict us, to them let us apply the remedy. If it is the delusiveness of things, whereby that appeareth to be good which is not so, to that let us seek for the remedy. If a habit afflicts us, against that must we endeavour to find some remedy. And what remedy is to be found against a habit? The contrary habit. Thou hearest the ignorant when they say, *The wretched man is dead; his father is perishing with grief for him, or his mother; he was cut off, yea, and untimely, and in a strange land.* Hearken, then, to the contrary words. Tear thyself away from such utterances. Against habit set the contrary habit. Against the words of the Sophists have the maxims of philosophers and the exercise and constant usage of them; against the delusiveness of things have clear natural conceptions ever burnished and ready.

3. Whenever death may appear to be an evil, have ready the thought that it is right to avoid evils, and that death is unavoidable. For what shall I do? whither shall I flee from it? Let it be granted that I am no Sarpedon, son of Zeus, to speak in that lofty style: *I go, either to do great deeds myself, or to give another the chance of doing them; though I myself fail I shall not grudge it to another to do nobly.*[2] Let it be granted that this is above us; still can we not at least rise to the height of that? And whither shall I flee from death? declare to me the place; declare to me the men among whom I shall go, to whom death comes never near; declare to me the charms against it. If I have none, what would ye have me do? I

cannot escape death—shall I not then escape the fear of death? shall I die lamenting and trembling? In this is the source of suffering, to wish for something, and that it should not come to pass; and thence it is that when I am able to alter outward things at my desire, I do so, but when not, I am ready to tear out the eyes of him that hindereth me. For man is so made by nature that he will not bear to be deprived of the Good nor to fall into the Evil. And in the end, when I am neither able to alter outward things nor to tear out the eyes of him that hindereth me, I sit down and groan and rail on whomsoever I can, Zeus and the other Gods;—for if they neglect me, what have I to do with them? *Yea, but thou wilt be an impious man.* And how shall I be worse off than I am now? Here is the whole matter: Remember that unless religion and profit meet in the same thing, religion cannot be saved in any man. Do not these things mightily convince of their truth?

4. Let the Pyrrhonist and the Academic come and make their attack—I, for my part, have no leisure for such discussions, nor am I able to argue in defence of general consent.³ For if I had a suit about a little piece of land, would I not call in another to argue for me? Wherewith shall I be satisfied? With that which concerns the matter in hand. How perception takes place, whether by the whole man or by parts, perhaps I know not how to declare: both opinions perplex me. But that thou and I are not the same I know very clearly. *Whence know you this?* Never, when I wish to eat, do I carry the morsel to

another man's mouth, but to my own. Never, when I wish to take a piece of bread, do I lay hold of a broom, but I always go to the bread, as to a mark. And ye who deny the truth of perception, what do ye other than I? Which of you, desiring to go to the bath, ever went into a mill? *What then? Ought we not, according to our abilities, to busy ourselves with the upholding of general consent, and raising defences against all that opposeth the same?* And who denies it? But let him do it that can, that hath leisure; but he that trembleth, and is troubled and his heart is broken within him, let him spend his time on something different.

## CHAPTER VIII.

### HOW WE SHOULD THINK AS GOD'S OFFSPRING.

1. IF those things are true which are said by philosophers concerning the kinship of God and men, what else remains for men to do than after Socrates' way, who never, when men inquired of him what was his native country, replied <u>Athens or Corinth, but the universe</u>. For why wilt thou say thou art an Athenian, and not rather name thyself from that nook alone into which thy wretched body was cast at birth? Is it not plainly from the lordlier place, and that which contains not only that nook and all thy household, but also the whole land whence the

race of thy ancestors has come down even to thee, that thou callest thyself Athenian or Corinthian? Whoso, therefore, hath watched the governance of the universe, and hath learned that the greatest and mightiest and amplest of all societies is that which is composed of mankind and of God; and that from Him have descended the seeds not only to my father alone, nor to my grandfather, but to all creatures that are conceived and born upon the earth (but especially to reasoning beings, since to these alone hath nature given it to have communion and intercourse with God, being linked with Him through Reason),—wherefore should such a one not name himself a citizen of the universe; wherefore not a son of God? wherefore shall he fear anything that may come to pass among men? And shall kinship with Cæsar, or with some other of those that are mighty at Rome, be enough to let us live in safety and undespised and fearing nothing at all; but to have God for our maker and father and guardian, shall this not avail to deliver us from griefs and fears?

*But I have no money*, saith one; *whence shall I have bread to eat?*

2. Art thou not ashamed to be more cowardly and spiritless than fugitive slaves are? How do they leave their masters when they run away? in what estates do they put their trust? in what servants? After stealing a little to serve them for the first few days, do they not afterwards journey by land and sea, and make their living by one device after another? And when did ever any fugitive

slave die of hunger? But thou tremblest and sleepest not of nights, for fear lest the necessaries of life fail thee. Wretched man! art thou thus blind? and seest not the road whither the want of necessaries leads a man? And whither leads it? To the same place that a fever doth, or a falling rock—to death. Hast thou not often said this to thy friends? and often read aloud these things, and written them? and how often hast thou vaunted thyself that thou wert at peace about death? *Yea, but my dear ones shall also suffer hunger.* What then? Doth their hunger lead to any other place than thine? Do they not descend where thou descendest? Is there not one underworld for them and thee? Wilt thou not, then, be bold in all poverty and need, looking to that place whither the wealthiest of men, and the mightiest governors, yea, and even kings and tyrants, must go down; thou, it may be, an-hungered, and they bursting with indigestion and drunkenness?

How seldom is it that a beggar is seen that is not an old man, and even of exceeding age? but freezing by night and day, and lying on the ground, and eating only what is barely necessary, they come near to being unable to die. Canst thou not transcribe writings? canst thou not teach children? or be some man's door-keeper?

*But it is shameful to come to such a necessity!*

Then first of all learn what things are shameful, and afterwards tell us thou art a philosopher. But at present suffer not even another man to call thee so.

3. Is that shameful to thee which is not thine

own doing, whereof thou art not the cause, which cometh to thee without thy will, like a headache or a fever? If thy parents were poor, or made others their heirs, or are alive and give thee nothing, are these things shameful to thee? Is this what thou hast learned from the philosophers? Hast thou never heard that what is shameful is blamable; and that which is blamable ought to be blamed? But what man wilt thou blame for a work not his own, one that he himself never did? And didst thou make thy father such as he is? or was it in thy power to correct him?—is it given thee to do this? What then? Oughtest thou to desire what is not given to thee? or to be ashamed if thou attain it not? Or hast thou been accustomed, in philosophy, to look to others, and to hope for nothing from thyself? Lament, therefore, and groan, and eat thy bread in fear, lest thou have nothing to eat on the morrow. Tremble for thy slaves, lest they steal, or run away, or die. Do thou live thus, now and ever, who hast approached to the name only of philosophy, and hast brought the precepts of it to shame, so far as in thee lies, showing them to be worthless and useless to those who adopt them; thou, who hast never striven to gain steadfastness, tranquillity, peace; that never waited upon any man for the sake of these things, but upon many for the sake of learning syllogisms; that never tested for thine own self any one of these appearances:—*Am I able to bear it, or am I not able? What, then, remains for me to do?* But, as though all went fairly and safely with thee, thou abidest in the final part of philosophy,[1] that which confirms beyond all change—and wherein wilt thou be confirmed? in cowardice, meanness, admiration of wealth, in vain pursuit, and vain efforts to avoid? These are the things thou dost meditate how to preserve unharmed.

4. Shouldst thou not have first have gained something from Reason, and then fortified this with safety? Whom sawest thou ever building a coping round about, and never a wall on which to place it? And what door-keeper is set on guard where there is no door? But thy study is how to prove propositions—and *what* proposition? How the billows of false reasonings may sweep thee not away—and away from *what?* Show me first what thing thou art guarding, or measuring, or weighing; and afterwards the scales or the measuring-rod. Or how long wilt thou still be measuring the dust? Are not these the things it behoves thee to prove:—what it is that makes men happy, what makes things proceed as we would have them, how one should blame no man, accuse no man, and fit oneself to the ordering of the All? Yea, prove me these! *But I do so*, he saith. *See! I resolve you syllogisms.* Slave! this is the measuring-rod—it is not the thing measured. Wherefore now you pay the penalty for philosophy neglected; you tremble, you lie awake at nights, you seek counsel on every hand, and if the counsels are not pleasing to all men, you think they were ill-counselled.

5. Then you fear hunger, as you suppose. But it is not hunger that you fear—you fear you will have

no cook, nor nobody else to buy victuals for you, nor another to take off your boots, nor another to put them on, nor others to rub you down, nor others to follow you about, so that when you have stripped yourself in the bath, and stretched yourself out as if you were crucified, you may be rubbed to and fro, and then the rubber standing by may say, *Turn him round, give me his side, take hold of his head, let me have his shoulder;* and then when you leave the bath and go home you may shout, *Is no one bringing anything to eat?* and then, *Take away the plates, and wipe them.* This is what you fear,—lest you be not able to live like a sick man. But learn how those live that are in health—slaves, and labourers, and true philosophers; how Socrates lived, who moreover had a wife and children; how Diogenes lived; how Cleanthes, that studied in the schools and drew his own water.[2] If you would have these things, they are everywhere to be had, and you will live boldly. Bold in what? In that wherein alone it is possible to be bold—in that which is faithful, which cannot be hindered, which cannot be taken away. But why hast thou made thyself so worthless and useless that no one is willing to receive thee into his house or take care of thee? But if any utensil were thrown away, and it was sound and serviceable, everyone that found it would pick it up and think it a gain; but thee no man would pick up, nor count anything but damage. So thou canst not so much as serve the purpose of a watch-dog, or a cock? Why, then, wilt thou still live, being such a man as thou art?

## HOW WE SHOULD THINK. 69

6. Doth any good man fear lest the means of gaining food fail him? They fail not the blind, nor the lame; shall they fail a good man? To the good soldier there fails not one who gives him pay, nor to the labourer, nor to the shoemaker; and shall such a one fail to the good man? Is God, then, careless of His instruments, His servants, His witnesses, whom alone He useth to show forth to the untaught what He is, and that He governs all things well, and is not careless of human things? and that to a good man there is no evil, neither in life nor in death? *How, then, when He leaves them without food?* How else is this than as when a good general gives me the signal for retreat? I obey, I follow, praising my leader and hymning his works. For I came when it pleased him, and when it pleases him I will go. In my lifetime also my work was to sing the praise of God, both alone to myself, and to single persons, and in presence of many. He doth not provide me with many things, nor with great abundance of goods; He will not have me live delicately. For neither did He provide so for Hercules, His own son, but another man reigned over Argos and Mycenæ, while he obeyed and laboured and was disciplined. And Eurystheus was what he was—no king of Argos and Mycenæ, who was not king even of himself; and Hercules was lord and leader of all the earth and sea, for he purged them of lawlessness and wrong, and brought in righteousness and holiness; naked and alone did he this. And when Odysseus was shipwrecked and cast away, did his need humble him one whit or

break his spirit? But how did he go out to the maidens, to beg for the necessaries of life, which it is held most shameful to seek from another?

> "Even as a lion from his mountain home,
> So went Odysseus trusting in his valour."
> —*Odyssey*, vi. 130.

Trusting in what? Not in fame, nor wealth, but in his own valour—that is, his opinions of the things that are and are not in our power.[3] For these alone it is that make men free and unhindered; that lift up the heads of the abject, and bid them look rich men and tyrants steadily in the face. And this was the gift of the philosopher; but thou wilt never go forth boldly, but trembling for thy fine raiment and silver dishes. Miserable man! hast thou indeed thus wasted all thy time till now?

---

## CHAPTER IX.

### THE OPEN DOOR.

1. For my part I think the old man should be sitting here, not to devise how ye may have no mean thoughts, nor speak no mean nor ignoble things about yourselves, but to watch that there arise not among us youths of such a mind, that when they have perceived their kinship with the Gods, and how the flesh and its possessions are

laid upon us like bonds, and how many necessities for the management of life are by them brought upon us, they may desire to fling these things away for abhorred and intolerable intolerable burthens, and depart unto their kin. And this is what your master and teacher —if, in sooth, ye had any such—should have to contend with in you,—that ye should come to him and say, *Epictetus, we can endure no longer being bound to this body, giving it food and drink, and resting it and cleansing it, and going about to court one man after another for its sake. Are not such things indifferent and nothing to us? And is not Death no evil? Are we not in some way kinsmen of God, and did we not come from him? Let us depart to whence we came; let us be delivered at last from these bonds wherewith we are bound and burthened! Here are robbers, and thieves, and law courts, and those that are called tyrants, which through the body and its possessions seem as if they had some power over us. Let us show them that they have no power over any man!* And to this it should be my part to say, "My friends, wait upon God. When He himself shall give the signal and release you from this service, then are ye released unto Him. But for the present, bear to dwell in this place, wherein He has set you. Short, indeed, is this time of your sojourn, and easy to bear for those that are so minded. For what tyrant or what thief is there any longer, or what court of law is terrible to one who thus makes nothing of the body and the possessions of it? Remain, then, and depart not without a reason." Some such part as this should the teacher have to play towards the well-natured among his disciples.

2. How long, then, are such injunctions to be obeyed? So long as it is profitable—that is to say, so long as I can do what becomes and befits me. Then some men are choleric and fastidious, and say, "I cannot sup with this man, to have to hear him every day telling how he fought in Mysia." *I told you, brother, how I went up the hill—then again I began to be besieged. . . .* But another saith, "I prefer to have my supper, and listen to him prating as long as he likes." And do thou compare the gain on both sides—only do naught in heaviness or affliction, or as supposing that thou art in evil case. For to this no man can compel thee. Doth it smoke in the chamber? if it is not very much I will stay, if too much, I will go out; for remember this always, and hold fast to it, that the door is open. *Thou shalt not live in Nicopolis.* I will not. *Nor in Athens.* I will not live in Athens. *Nor in Rome.* Neither in Rome. *Live in Gyara.*[1] I will live in Gyara. But living in Gyara seemeth to me like a great smoke. I will depart, whither no man shall hinder me to dwell —for that dwelling stands ever open to all.

3. Only do it not unreasonably, nor cowardly, nor make every common chance an excuse. For again, it is not God's will, for He hath need of such an order of things, and of such a race upon the earth. But if He give the signal for retreat, as He did to Socrates, we must obey Him as our commander.

## CHAPTER X.

KNOW THYSELF.

1. IF a man have any advantage over others, or think himself to have it when he hath it not, it cannot but be that if he is an untaught man he shall be puffed up by it. Thus the tyrant says, *I am he that is master of all.* And what can you give me? Can you set my pursuit free of all hindrance? How is it in you to do that? For have you the gift of never falling into what you shun? or never missing the mark of your desire? And whence have you it? Come, now, in a ship do you trust to yourself or to the captain? or in a chariot, to anyone else than the driver? And how will you do with regard to other acts? Even thus. Where, then, is your power? *All men minister to me.* And do I not minister to my plate, and I wash it and wipe it, and drive in a peg for my oil-flask? What then, are these things greater than I? Nay, but they supply certain of my needs, and for this reason I take care of them. Yea, and do I not minister to my ass? Do I not wash his feet and groom him? Know you not that every man ministers to himself? And he ministers to you also, even as he doth to the ass. For who treats you as a man? Show me one that doth. Who wisheth to be like unto you? who becomes your imitator, as men did of Socrates? *But I can cut off thy head.* You say well. I had forgotten that I must pay regard to you as to a fever

or the cholera; and set up an altar to you, as there is in Rome an altar to Fever.

2. What is it, then, whereby the multitude is troubled and terrified? The tyrant and his guards? Never—God forbid it! It is not possible that that which is by nature free should be troubled by any other thing, or hindered, save by itself. But it is troubled by opinions of things. For when the tyrant saith to anyone, *I will bind thy leg*, then he who setteth store by his leg saith, *Nay, have pity!* but he that setteth store by his own Will, *If it seem more profitable to you, then bind it.*

——"Dost thou not regard me?"

I do not regard you. I will show you that I am master. How can you be that? Me hath God set free; or think you that he would let his own son be enslaved? You are lord of my dead body—take that.

——"So when thou comest near to me, thou wilt not do me service?"

Nay, but I will do it to myself; and if you will have me say that I do it to you also, I tell you that I do it as to my kitchen pot.

3. This is no selfishness; for every living creature is so made that it doth all things for its own sake. For the sun doth all things for his own sake, and so, moreover, even Zeus himself. But when He will be Raingiver and Fruitgiver and Father of Gods and men, thou seest that He may not do these works and have these titles, but He be serviceable to the common good. And, on the whole, He hath so formed the

# KNOW THYSELF. 75

nature of the reasoning creature that he may never win aught of his own good without he furnish something of service to the common good. Thus it is not to the excluding of the common good that a man do all things for himself. For is it to be expected that a man shall stand aloof from himself and his own interest? And where then would be that same and single principle which we observe in all things, their affection to themselves?

4. So, then, when we act on strange and foolish opinions of things beyond the Will, as though they were good or evil, it is altogether impossible but we shall do service to tyrants. And would it were to the tyrants alone, and not to their lackeys also!

5. But what hinders the man that hath distinguished these things to live easily and docile, looking calmly on all that is to be, and bearing calmly all that is past? Will you have me bear poverty? Come, and see what poverty is when it strikes one that knoweth how to play the part well. Will you have me rule? Give me power, then, and the pains of it. Banishment? Whithersoever I go, it shall be well with me; for in this place it was well with me, not because of the place, but because of the opinions which I shall carry away with me. For these no man can deprive me of. Yea, these only are mine own, whereof I cannot be deprived, and they suffice for me as long as I have them, wherever I be, or whatever I do.

6. ——"But now is the time come to die." What say you? to die? Nay, make no tragedy of

the business, but tell it as it is.  Now is it time for my substance to be resolved again into the things wherefrom it came together.  And what is dreadful in this? What of the things in the universe is about to perish? What new, or what unaccountable thing is about to come to pass?  Is it for these things that a tyrant is feared? through these that the guards seem to bear swords so large and sharp?  Tell that to others; but by me all these things have been examined; no man hath power on me.  I have been set free by God, I know His commandments, henceforth no man can lead me captive.  I have a liberator[2] such as I need, and judges such as I need.  Are you not the master of my body?  What is that to me?  Of my property? What is that to me?  Of exile or captivity?  Again, I say, from all these things, and the poor body itself, I will depart when you will.  Try your power, and you shall know how far it reaches.

7. But the tyrant will bind—what?  The leg. He will take away—what?  The head.  What, then, can he not bind and not take away?  The Will.  And hence that precept of the ancients—KNOW THYSELF.

8. Whom, then, can I still fear?  The lackeys of the bed-chamber?  For what that they can do?  Shut me out?  Let them shut me out, if they find me wishing to go in.

——" Why, then, didst thou go to the doors?"

Because I hold it proper to join the play while the play lasts.

——" How, then, shalt thou not be shut out?"

Because if I am not received, I do not wish to enter; but always that which happens is what I wish. For I hold what God wills above what I will. I cleave to Him as His servant and follower; my impulses are one with His, my pursuit is one with His; in a word, my will is one with His. There is no shutting out for me—nay, but for those who would force their way in. And wherefore do I not force my way? Because I know that no good thing is dealt out within to those that enter. But when I hear some one congratulated on being honoured by Cæsar, I say, What hath fortune brought him? A government? Has it also, then, brought him such an opinion as he ought to have? A magistracy? Hath he also gained the power to be a good magistrate? Why will I still push myself forward? A man scatters figs and almonds abroad; children seize them, and fight among themselves; but not so men, for they hold it too trifling a matter. And if a man should scatter about oyster-shells, not even the children would seize them. Offices of government are dealt out—children will look for them; money is given—children will look for it; military commands, consulships—let children scramble for them. Let them be shut out and smitten, let them kiss the hands of the giver, of his slaves—it is figs and almonds to me. What then? If thou miss them when he is flinging them about, let it not vex thee. If a fig fall into thy bosom, take and eat it, for so far even a fig is to be valued. But if I must stoop down for it, and throw down another man, or another throw me down, and I flatter those who enter in, then neither is a fig worth so much, nor is any other of the things that are not good, even those which the philosophers have persuaded me not to think good.

## CHAPTER XI.[1]

#### HOW WE SHOULD BEAR OURSELVES TOWARDS EVIL MEN.

1. IF that which the philosophers say is true—that there is one principle in all men, as when I assent to something, the feeling that it is so; and when I dissent, the feeling that it is not so; yea, and when I withhold my judgment, the feeling that it is uncertain; and likewise, when I am moved towards anything, the feeling that it is for my profit, but it is impossible to judge one thing to be profitable and to pursue another, to judge one thing right and be moved towards another—why have we indignation with the multitude? *They are robbers*, one saith, *and thieves.* And what is it to be robbers and thieves? It is to err concerning things good and evil. Shall we, then, have indignation with them, or shall we pity them? Nay, but show them the error, and you shall see how they will cease from their sins. But if they see it not, they have naught better than the appearance of the thing to them.

2. *Should not, then, this robber, or this adulterer, be destroyed?* By no means, but take it rather this

way: *This man who errs and is deceived concerning things of greatest moment, who is blinded, not in the vision which distinguisheth black and white, but in the judgment which distinguisheth Good and Evil—should we not destroy him?* And thus speaking, you shall know how inhuman is that which you say, and how like as if you said, *Shall we not destroy this blind man, this deaf man?* For if it is the greatest injury to be deprived of the greatest things, and the greatest thing in every man is a Will such as he ought to have, and one be deprived of this, why are you still indignant with him? Man, you should not be moved contrary to Nature by the evil deeds of other men. Pity him rather, be not inclined to offence and hatred, abandon the phrases of the multitude, like "these cursed wretches." How have you suddenly become so wise and hard to please?

3. Wherefore, then, have we indignation? Because we worship the things which they deprive us of. Do not worship fine raiment, and you shall not be wroth with the thief. Do not worship the beauty of a woman, and you shall not be wroth with the adulterer. Know that the thief and the adulterer have no part in that which is thine own, but in that which is foreign to thee, in that which is not in thy power. These things if thou dismiss, and count them for naught, with whom shalt thou still be wroth? But so long as thou dost value these things, be wroth with thyself rather than with others.

4. Look now how it stands: You have fine raiment, your neighbour has not; you have a window, and

wish to air your clothes at it. The neighbour knoweth not what is the true good of man, but thinks it is to have fine raiment, the same thing that you also think. Then shall he not come and take them away? Show a cake to greedy persons, and eat it up yourself alone, and will you have them not snatch at it? Nay, but provoke them not. Have no window, and do not air your clothes. I also had lately an iron lamp set beside the images of the Gods; hearing a noise at the door, I ran down, and found the lamp carried off. I reflected that the thief's impulse was not unnatural. What then? *To-morrow,* I said, *thou wilt find an earthen lamp.*² For a man loses only what he has. *I have lost a garment.* For you had a garment. *I have a pain in my head.* Have you any pain in your horns? Why, then, have you indignation? For there is no loss and no suffering save only in those things which we possess.

## CHAPTER XII.

### THE VOYAGE OF LIFE.

Even as in a sea voyage, when the ship is brought to anchor, and you go out to fetch in water, you make a by-work of gathering a few roots and shells by the way, but have need ever to keep your mind fixed on the ship, and constantly to look round, lest at any time the master of the ship call, and you must, if he call, cast away all those things, lest you be treated like the sheep that are bound and thrown into the hold: So it is with human life also. And if there be given wife and children instead of shells and roots, nothing shall hinder us to take them. But if the master call, run to the ship, forsaking all those things, and looking not behind. And if thou be in old age, go not far from the ship at any time, lest the master should call, and thou be not ready.

## CHAPTER XIII.

### THE MARK OF EFFORT.

1. SEEK not to have things happen as you choose them, but rather choose them to happen as they do, and so shall you live prosperously.

2. Disease is a hindrance of the body, not of the Will, unless the Will itself consent. Lameness is a hindrance of the leg, not of the Will. And this you may say on every occasion, for nothing can happen to you but you will find it a hindrance not of yourself but of some other thing.

3. What, then, are the things that oppress us and perturb us? What else than opinions? He that goeth away and leaveth his familiars and companions and wonted places and habits—with what else is he oppressed than his opinions? Now, little children, if they cry because their nurse has left them for a while,

straightway forget their sorrow when they are given a small cake. Wilt thou be likened unto a little child?

——"Nay, by Zeus! for I would not be thus affected by a little cake, but by right opinions."

And what are these?

They are such as a man should study all day long to observe—that he be not subject to the effects of any thing that is alien to him, neither of friend, nor place, nor exercises; yea, not even of his own body, but to remember the Law, and have it ever before his eyes. And what is the divine Law? To hold fast that which is his own, and to claim nothing that is another's; to use what is given him, and not to covet what is not given; to yield up easily and willingly what is taken away, giving thanks for the time that he has had it at his service. This do—or cry for the nurse and mamma; for what doth it matter to what or whom thou art subject, from what thy welfare hangs? Wherein art thou better than one who bewails himself for his mistress, if thou lament thy exercises and porticoes and comrades, and all such pastime? Another cometh, grieving because he shall no more drink of the water of Dirce. And is the Marcian water worse than that of Dirce?

——"But I was used to the other."

And to this also thou shalt be used; and when thou art so affected towards it, lament for it too, and try to make a verse like that of Euripides—

"The baths of Nero and the Marcian stream."[1]

## THE MARK OF EFFORT.

Behold how tragedies are made, when common chances happen to foolish men!

4. ——" But when shall I see Athens and the Acropolis again?"

Wretched man! doth not that satisfy thee which thou seest every day? Hast thou aught better or greater to see than the sun, the moon, the stars, the common earth, the sea? But if withal thou mark the way of Him that governeth the whole, and bear Him about within thee, wilt thou still long for cut stones and a fine rock? And when thou shalt come to leave the sun itself and the moon, what wilt thou do? Sit down and cry, like the children? What, then, wert thou doing in the school? What didst thou hear, what didst thou learn? Why didst thou write thyself down a philosopher, when thou mightest have written the truth, as thus:—*I made certain beginnings, and read Chrysippus, but did not so much as enter the door of a philosopher?* For how shouldst thou have aught in common with Socrates, who died as he died, who lived as he lived—or with Diogenes? Dost thou think that any of these men lamented or was indignant because he should see such a man or such a woman no more? or because he should not dwell in Athens or in Corinth, but, as it might chance, in Susa or Ecbatana? When a man can leave the banquet or the game when he pleases, shall such a one grieve if he remains? Shall he not, as in a game, stay only so long as he is entertained? A man of this stamp would easily endure such a thing as perpetual exile or sentence of death.

Wilt thou not now be weaned as children are, and take more solid food, nor cry any more after thy mother and nurse, wailing like an old woman?

——"But if I quit them I shall grieve them."

Thou grieve them? Never; but that shall grieve them which grieveth thee—Opinion. What hast thou, then, to do? Cast away thy own bad opinion; and they, if they do well, will cast away theirs; if not, they are the causes of their own lamenting.

5. Man, be mad at last, as the saying is, for peace, for freedom, for magnanimity. Lift up thy head, as one delivered from slavery. Dare to look up to God and say: *Deal with me henceforth as thou wilt; I am of one mind with thee; I am thine. I reject nothing that seems good to thee; lead me whithersoever thou wilt, clothe me in what dress thou wilt. Wilt thou have me govern or live privately, or stay at home, or go into exile, or be a poor man, or a rich? For all these conditions I will be thy advocate with men—I show the nature of each of them, what it is.*

Nay, but sit in a corner and wait for thy mother to feed thee.[2]

6. Who would Hercules have been if he had sat at home? He would have been Eurystheus, and not Hercules. And how many companions and friends had he in his journeying about the world? But nothing was dearer to him than God; and for this he was believed to be the son of God, yea, and was the son of God. And trusting in God, he went about purging away lawlessness and wrong. But thou art no Hercules, and canst not purge away evils not thine

own? nor yet Theseus, who cleared Attica of evil things? Then clear away thine own. From thy breast, from thy mind cast out, instead of Procrustes and Sciron, grief, fear, covetousness, envy, malice, avarice, effeminacy, profligacy. And these things cannot otherwise be cast out than by looking to God only, being affected only by him, and consecrated to his commands. But choosing anything else than this, thou wilt follow with groaning and lamentation whatever is stronger than thou, ever seeking prosperity in things outside thyself, and never able to attain it. For thou seekest it where it is not, and neglectest to seek it where it is.

## CHAPTER XIV.

### FACULTIES.

REMEMBER at anything that shall befall thee to turn to thyself and seek what faculty thou hast for making use of it. If thou see a beautiful person, thou wilt find a faculty for that—namely, self-mastery. If toil is laid upon thee, thou wilt find the faculty of Perseverance. If thou art reviled, thou wilt find Patience. And making this thy wont, thou shalt not be carried away by the appearances.

## CHAPTER XV.

### RETURNS.

NEVER in any case say, *I have lost* such a thing, but *I have returned it*? Is thy child dead? it is returned. Is thy wife dead? she is returned. Art thou deprived of thy estate? is not this also returned?

——" But he is wicked who deprives me of it!"

But what is that to thee, through whom the Giver demands his own? As long, therefore, as he grants it to thee, steward it like another's property, as travellers use an inn.

## CHAPTER XVI.

### THE PRICE OF TRANQUILLITY.

1. IF you would advance in philosophy you must abandon such thoughts as, *If I neglect my affairs I shall not have the means of living. If I do not correct my servant he will be good for nothing.* For it is better to die of hunger, having lived without grief and fear, than to live with a troubled spirit amid abundance. And it is better to have a bad servant than an afflicted mind.

2. Make a beginning, then, in small matters. Is a

little of your oil spilt, or a little wine stolen ? Then say to yourself, *For so much peace is bought, this is the price of tranquillity.* For nothing can be gained without paying for it. And when you call your servant, bethink you that he may not hear, or, hearing, may not obey. For him, indeed, that is not well, but for you it is altogether well that he have not the power to trouble your mind.

## CHAPTER XVII.

### A CHOICE.

If thou wouldst advance, be content to let people think thee senseless and foolish as regards external things. Wish not ever to seem wise, and if ever thou shalt find thyself accounted to be somebody, then mistrust thyself. For know that it is not easy to make a choice that shall agree both with outward things and with Nature, but it must needs be that he who is careful of the one shall neglect the other.

## CHAPTER XVIII.

### THAT WHERE THE HEART IS THE BOND IS.

1. THOU art a fool if thou desire wife and children and friends to live forever, for that is desiring things to be in thy power which are not in thy power, and things pertaining to others to be thine own. So also thou art a fool to desire that thy servant should never do anything amiss, for that is desiring evil not to be evil, but something else. But if thou desire never to fail in any pursuit, this thou canst do. This, therefore, practice to attain—namely, the attainable.

2. The lord of each of us is he that hath power over the things that we desire or dislike, to give or to take them away. Whosoever, then, will be free, let him neither desire nor shun any of the things that are in others' power; otherwise he must needs be enslaved.

3. Wherefore Demetrius[1] said to Nero, *You threaten me with death, but Nature threatens you.* If I am taken up with my poor body, or my property, I have given myself over to slavery; for I immediately show of my own self with what I may be captured. As when a snake draws in his head, I say, *Strike at that part of him which he guards.* And know thou, that at the part thou desirest to guard, there thy master will fall upon thee. Remembering this, whom wilt thou still flatter or fear?

4. Think that thou shouldst conduct thyself in life as at a feast. Is some dish brought to thee? Then

put forth thy hand and help thyself in seemly fashion. Doth it pass thee by? Then hold it not back. Hath it not yet come? Then do not reach out for it at a distance, but wait till it is at thine hand. And thus doing with regard to children and wife and governments and wealth, thou wilt be a worthy guest at the table of the Gods. And if thou even pass over things that are offered to thee, and refuse to take of them, then thou wilt not only share the banquet, but also the dominion of the Gods. For so doing Diogenes and Heracleitus, and the like, both were, and were reported to be, rightly divine.

## CHAPTER XIX.

### THAT WE LAMENT NOT FROM WITHIN.

WHEN thou seest one lamenting in grief because his son is gone abroad, or because he hath lost his goods, look to it that thou be not carried away by the appearance to think that he hath truly fallen into misfortune, in outward things. But be the thought at hand, *It is not the thing itself that afflicts this man —since there are others whom it afflicts not—but the opinion he has about it.* And so far as speech, be not slow to fit thyself to his mood, and even if so it be to lament with him. But have a care that thou lament not also from within.

## CHAPTER XX.

#### THAT A MAN MAY ACT HIS PART BUT NOT CHOOSE IT.

1. REMEMBER that thou art an actor in a play, of such a part as it may please the director to assign thee; of a short part if he choose a short part; of a long one if he choose a long. And if he will have thee take the part of a poor man or of a cripple, or a governor, or a private person, mayest thou act that part with grace! For thine it is to act well the allotted part, but to choose it is another's.

2. Say no more then *How will it be with me?* for however it be thou wilt settle it well, and the issue shall be fortunate. What would Hercules have been had he said, *How shall I contrive that a great lion may not appear to me, or a great boar, or a savage man?* And what hast thou to do with that? if a great boar appear, thou wilt fight the greater fight; if evil men, thou wilt clear the earth of them. *But if I die thus?* Thou wilt die a good man, in the accomplishing of a noble deed. For since we must by all means die, a man cannot be found but he will be doing somewhat, either tilling or digging or trading or governing, or having an indigestion or a diarrhœa. What wilt thou, then, that Death shall find thee doing? I, for my part, will choose some work, humane, beneficent, social, noble. But if I am not able to be found doing things of this greatness, then, at least, I will be doing that which none can hinder me to do, that which is given to me

to do—namely, correcting myself, bettering my faculty for making use of appearances, working out my peace, giving what is due in every obligation of life; and if I prosper so far, then entering upon the third topic of philosophy, which concerneth the security of judgments.

3. If Death shall find me in the midst of these studies, it shall suffice me if I can lift up my hands to God and say, *The means which thou gavest me for the perceiving of thy government, and for the following of the same, have I not neglected: so far as in me lies, I have not dishonoured thee. Behold how I have used my senses, and my natural conceptions. Have I ever blamed thee? was I ever offended at aught that happened, or did I desire it should happen otherwise? Did I ever desire to transgress my obligations? That thou didst beget me I thank thee for what thou gavest: I am content that I have used thy gifts so long. Take them again, and set them in what place thou wilt, for thine were all things, and thou gavest them me.*

4. Is it not enough to depart in this condition? and what life is better and fairer than one like this, and what end more happy?

## CHAPTER XXI.

### DISTINCTIONS.

1. WHEN a raven croaks you a bad omen, be not carried away by the appearance; but straightway distinguish with yourself and say, *None of these things bodes aught to myself, but either to this poor body or this wretched property of mine, or to my good repute, or to my children, or to my wife. But to me all omens are fortunate, if I choose to have it so. For whatever of these things may come to pass, it lies with me to have it serve me.*

2. You may be always victorious if you will never enter into any contest but where the victory depends upon yourself.

3. When you shall see a man honoured above others, or mighty in power, or otherwise esteemed, look to it that thou deem him not blessed, being carried away by the appearance. For if the essence of the Good be in those things that are in our own power, then neither envy nor jealousy have any place, nor thou thyself shalt not desire to be commander or prince or consul, but to be free. And to this there is one road—scorn of the things that are not in our own power.

4. Remember, it is not he that strikes or he that reviles that doth any man an injury, but the opinion about these things, that they are injurious. When, then, someone may provoke thee to wrath, know that it is thine own conception which hath provoked thee.

Strive, therefore, at the outset not to be carried away by the appearance; for if thou once gain time and delay, thou wilt more easily master thyself.

5. Death and exile, and all things that appear dreadful, let these be every day before thine eyes. But Death most of all; for so thou wilt neither despise nor too greatly desire any condition of life.

## CHAPTER XXII.

### THAT A MAN IS SUFFICIENT TO HIMSELF.

1. IF thou set thine heart upon philosophy, prepare straightway to be laughed at and mocked by many who will say, *Behold, he has suddenly come back to us a philosopher;* or, *How came you by that brow of scorn?* But do thou cherish no scorn, but hold to those things that seem to thee the best, as one set by God in that place. Remember, too, that if thou abide in that way, those that first mocked thee, the same shall afterwards reverence thee; but if thou yield to them, thou shalt receive double mockery.

2. If it shall ever happen to thee to be turned to outward things in the desire to please some person, know that thou hast lost thy way of life. Let it be enough for thee in all things to *be* a philosopher. But if thou desire also to seem one, then seem so to thyself, for this thou canst.

## CHAPTER XXIII.

#### THAT EVERY MAN FULFIL HIS OWN TASK.

1. LET such thoughts never afflict thee as, *I shall live unhonoured, and never be anybody anywhere.* For if lack of honour be an evil, thou canst no more fall into evil through another's doings than into vice. Is it, then, of thy own doing to be made a governor, or invited to feasts? By no means. How, then, is this to be unhonoured? How shouldst thou *never be anybody anywhere*, whom it behoves to be somebody only in the things that are in thine own power, wherein it lies with thee to be of the greatest worth?

2. *But I shall not be able to serve my friends.* How sayst thou? to serve them? They shall not have money from thee, nor shalt thou make them Roman citizens. Who, then, told thee that these were of the things that are in our power, and not alien to us? And who can give that which himself hath not?

3. *Acquire, then,* they say, *that we may possess.* If I can acquire, and lose not piety, and faith, and magnanimity withal, show me the way, and I will do it. But if ye will have me lose the good things I possess, that ye may compass things that are not good at all, how unjust and unthinking are ye! But which will ye rather have—money, or a faithful and pious friend? Then, rather take part with me to this end; and ask me not to do aught through which I must cast away those things.

4. *But*, he saith, *I shall not do my part in serving my country.* Again, what is this service? Thy country shall not have porticos nor baths from thee, and what then? Neither hath she shoes from the smith, nor arms from the cobbler; but it is enough if every man fulfil his own task. And if thou hast made one other pious and faithful citizen for her, art thou, then, of no service? Wherefore, neither shalt thou be useless to thy country.

5. *What place, then,* he saith, *can I hold in the State?* Whatever place thou canst, guarding still thy faith and piety. But if in wishing to serve her thou cast away these things, what wilt thou profit her then, when perfected in shamelessness and faithlessness?


CHAPTER XXIV.

THE WORLD'S PRICE FOR THE WORLD'S WORTH.

1. Is some one preferred before thee at a feast, or in salutation, or in being invited to give counsel? Then, if these things are good, it behoves thee rejoice that he hath gained them; but if evil, be not vexed that thou hast not gained them; but remember that if thou act not as other men to gain the things that are not in our own power, neither canst thou be held worthy of a like reward with them.

2. For how is it possible for him who will not hang about other men's doors to have a like reward with him who doth so? or him who will not attend on them with him who doth attend? or him who will not flatter them with the flatterer? Thou art unjust, then, and insatiable, if thou desire to gain those things for nothing, without paying the price for which they are sold.

3. But how much is a lettuce sold for? A penny, perchance. If anyone, then, will spend a penny, he shall have lettuce; but thou, not spending, shalt not have. But think not thou art worse off than he; for as he has the lettuce, so thou the penny which thou wouldst not give.

4. And likewise in this matter. Thou art not invited to some man's feast? That is, for thou gavest not to the host the price of the supper; and it is sold for flattery, it is sold for attendance. Pay, then, the price, if it will profit thee, for which the thing is sold. But if thou wilt not give the price, and wilt have the thing, greedy art thou and infatuated.

5. Shalt thou have nothing, then, instead of the supper? Thou shalt have this—not to have praised one whom thou hadst no mind to praise, and not to have endured the insolence of his door-keepers.

## CHAPTER XXV.

#### AIMS OF NATURE.

1. THE will of Nature is to be learned from matters which do not concern ourselves.[1] Thus, when a boy may break the cup of another man, we are ready to say, *It is a common chance.* Know, then, that when thine own is broken, it behoves thee to be as though it were another man's. And apply this even to greater things. Has another man's child died, or his wife? who is there that will not say, *It is the lot of humanity.* But when his own may die, then straightway it is, *Alas, wretched that I am!* But we should bethink ourselves what we felt on hearing of others in the same plight.

2. As a mark is not set up to be missed, even so the nature of evil exists not in the universe.

---

## CHAPTER XXVI.

#### THE MIND'S SECURITY.

IF anyone should set your body at the mercy of every passer-by, you would be indignant. When, therefore, you set your own mind at the mercy of every chance, to be troubled and perturbed when anyone may revile you, have you no shame of this?

## CHAPTER XXVII.

#### THAT A MAN SHOULD BE ONE MAN.

1. In every work you will take in hand mark well what must go before and what must follow, and so proceed. For else you shall at first set out eagerly, as not regarding what is to follow; but in the end, if any difficulties have arisen, you will leave it off with shame.

2. So you wish to conquer in the Olympic games? And I, too, by the Gods; and a fine thing it would be. But mark the prefaces and the consequences, and then set to work. You must go under discipline, eat by rule, abstain from dainties, exercise yourself at the appointed hour, in heat or cold, whether you will or no, drink nothing cold, nor wine at will; in a word, you must give yourself over to the trainer as to a physician. Then in the contest itself there is the digging race,[1] and you are like enough to dislocate your wrist, or turn your ankle, to swallow a great deal of dust, to be soundly drubbed, and after all these things to be defeated.

3. If, having considered these things, you are still in the mind to enter for the contest, then do so. But without consideration you will turn from one thing to another like a child, who now plays the wrestler, now the gladiator, now sounds the trumpet, then declaims like an actor; and so you, too, will be first an

athlete, then a gladiator, then an orator, then a philosopher, and nothing with your whole soul; but as an ape you will mimic everything you see, and be charmed with one thing after another. For you approached nothing with consideration nor regularity, but rashly, and with a cold desire.

4. And thus some men, having seen a philosopher, and heard discourse like that of Euphrates[2] (yet who indeed can say that any discourse is like his?) desire that they also may become philosophers.

5. But, O man! consider first what it is you are about to do, and then inquire of your own nature whether you can carry it out. Will you be a pentathlos,[3] or a wrestler? Then, scan your arms and thighs; try your loins. For different men are made for different ends.

6. Think you, you can be a sage, and continue to eat and drink and be wrathful and take offence just as you were wont? Nay, but you must watch and labour, and withdraw yourself from your household, and be despised by any serving boy, and be ridiculed by your neighbours, and take the lower place everywhere, in honours, in authority, in courts of justice, in dealings of every kind.[4]

7. Consider these things—whether you are willing at such a price to gain peace, freedom, and an untroubled spirit. And if not, then attempt it not, nor, like a child, play now the philosopher, then the tax-gatherer, then the orator, then the Procurator of Cæsar. For these things agree not among themselves; and, good or bad, it behoves you to be one

man. You should be perfecting either your own ruling faculty, or your outward well-being; spending your art either on the life within or the life without; that is to say, you must hold your place either among the sages or the vulgar.

END OF BOOK II.

# BOOK III.

## CHAPTER I.

### OBLIGATIONS.

1. OBLIGATIONS are universally defined by the bonds of relation. Is such a man your father? Then it is implied that you are to take care of him, to give place to him in all things, to bear his rebukes, his chastisement. *But if he be a bad father?* Were you then related by any law of Nature to a good father? Nay, but simply to a father. Your brother does you wrong. Then guard your own place towards him, nor scrutinise what he is doing, but what you may do to keep your will in accord with Nature. For none other shall hurt you, if yourself choose it not, but you shall be hurt then when you conceive yourself to be so.

2. Thus shall you discover your obligations from the offices of a neighbour, a citizen, a general, if you will accustom yourself to watch the relationships.

## CHAPTER II.

#### AGAINST EPICURUS.

1. EVEN Epicurus is conscious that we are by nature social, but having once placed the Good in the husk,[1] he cannot thereafter speak anything but what agrees with this; for again he affirms, and rightly affirms, that nothing is to be admired or received that is separated from the nature of the Good. How then, Epicurus, do you suspect that we are social, if Nature had given us no affection for our offspring?[2] Wherefore do you counsel the sage against bringing up children? Why do you fear lest he fall into sorrow by so doing? Doth he fall into sorrow for the mouse that lives in his house? What careth he if a little mouse complain to him at home. But he knows well that if a little child be born, it is no longer in our power not to love it and be anxious for it.

2. Thus, too, he saith that no man of sense will take part in affairs of the state, for he knows what he who takes part in them must do; but what should hinder one to take part, if he may behave among men as in a swarm of flies? But Epicurus, knowing these things, dares to say that we should not rear up our children. But even a sheep will not desert its young, nor a wolf; and shall a man? *What! will you have us to be silly creatures, like the sheep?* Yet they desert not their young. *Or savage, like wolves?* Yet even they desert them not. Come, then, who

would obey you if he saw his little child fall on the ground and cry? For my part, I suppose that had it been prophesied to your mother and your father that you would say these things, not even so would they have cast you out.

3. *But how can it be said of these outward things[3] that they are according to Nature, or contrary to Nature?* That is to speak as if we were solitary and disunited from others. For to the foot I shall say it is according to Nature that it be clean; but if you take it as a foot, and not as a solitary thing, it shall beseem it to go into the mud, and to tread on thorns, and perchance to be cut off, for the sake of the whole; otherwise it is no longer a foot.

4. And some such thing we should suppose about ourselves also. What art thou? A man. Look at thyself as a solitary creature, and it is according to Nature to live to old age, to grow rich, to keep good health. But if thou look at thyself as a man, and as a part of a certain Whole, for the sake of that Whole it may become thee now to have sickness, now to sail the seas and run into peril, now to suffer need, and perchance to die before thy time.

5. Why, then, dost thou bear it hard? Knowest thou not, that as the foot alone is not a foot, so thou alone art not a man? For what is a man? A part of a polity, first of that which is made up of Gods and men; then of that which is said to be next to the other, which is a small copy of the Universal Polity.

6. *Then must I now be brought to trial, and now must another have a fever, and another sail the seas,*

*another die, another be sentenced?* Yea, for with such a body, in the bounds of such a universe, in such a throng of inhabitants, it cannot be but that different things of this nature should fall on different persons. This is thy task then, having come into the world, to speak what thou shouldst, and to order these things as it is fitting.

7. Then someone saith, *I charge you with wrongdoing.* Much good may it do thee! I have done my part—look to it thyself if thou have done thine, for of this too there is some danger, lest it escape thee.

## CHAPTER III.

### AGAINST THE EPICUREANS AND ACADEMICS.

1. BELIEFS which are sound and manifestly true are of necessity used even by those who deny them. And perhaps a man might adduce this as the greatest possible proof of the manifest truth of anything, that those who deny it are compelled to make use of it. Thus, if a man should deny that there is anything universally true, it is clear that he is obliged to affirm the contrary, the negation—that there is nothing universally true. Slave! not even this—for what is this but to say that if there is anything universal it is falsehood?

2. Again, if one should come and say, *Know that*

*nothing can be known, but all things are incapable of proof;* or another, *Believe me, and it shall profit thee, that no man ought to believe any man;* or, again, another, *Learn from me, O man, that it is not possible to learn anything, and I tell thee this, and I will teach thee, if thou wilt*—now wherein do such men differ from those—whom shall I say?—those who call themselves Academics? *Assent, O men, that no man can assent to aught; believe us that no man can believe any one.*

3. Thus Epicurus, when he would abolish the natural fellowship of men with one another, employeth the very thing that is being abolished. For what saith he? *Be not deceived, O men, nor misguided nor mistaken—there is no natural fellowship among reasoning beings, believe me; and those who speak otherwise deceive us with sophisms.* What is that to thee? let us be deceived! Will it be the worse for thee if all other men are persuaded that we have a natural fellowship with one another, and that we should in all ways maintain it? Nay—but much the better and safer. Man, why dost thou take thought for us, and watch at night for our sakes? Why dost thou kindle thy lamp and rise early? why dost thou write so many books, lest any of us should be deceived about the Gods, in supposing that they cared for men? or lest anyone should take the essence of the Good to be anything else than Pleasure? For if these things are so, then lie down and sleep, and live the life of a worm, wherefor thou hast judged thyself fit; eat and drink and cohabit and ease thyself and snore.

What is it to thee how other men think concerning these matters, whether soundly or unsoundly? What hast thou to do with us? With sheep hast thou some concern, for that they serve us when they are shorn, and when they are milked, and at last when they have their throats cut. Were it not, then, to be desired, if men could be lulled and charmed to slumber by the Stoics, and give themselves to thee and the like of thee, to be shorn and milked? These things shouldst thou say to thy brother Epicureans; but shouldst thou not keep them hidden from other men, and seek in every way to persuade them above all things that we are by nature social, and that temperance is good; in order that everything may be kept for thee? Or should we preserve this fellowship with some and not with others? With whom, then, should we preserve it? With those who also preserve it towards us, or with those who transgress it? And who transgress it more than ye, who set forth such doctrines?

4. What, then, was it that roused up Epicurus from his sleep, and compelled him to write the things he wrote? What else than Nature, the mightiest of all powers in humanity? Nature, that drags the man, reluctant and groaning, to her will. *For*, saith she, *since it seems to thee that there is no fellowship among men, write this down, and deliver it to others, and watch and wake for this, and be thyself by thine own deed the accuser of thine own opinions.* Shall we then, say that Orestes was driven by the Furies and

aroused from sleep, and did not crueller Furies and Avengers rouse this man as he slumbered, and suffered him not to rest, but compelled him, as madness and wine the priests of Cybele,[1] to proclaim his own evils? So mighty and invincible a thing is man's nature.

5. For how can a vine be affected, and not in the nanner of a vine, but of an olive? Or how, again, can an olive be affected not in the manner of an olive but of a vine? It is impossible, it cannot be conceived. Neither, then, is it possible for a man wholly to lose the affections of humanity, for even eunuchs cannot cut away from themselves the desires of men. And thus Epicurus has cut away all that belongs to a man as father of a family, and as citizen, and as friend; but the desires of humanity he hath not cut away, for he could not; no more than these pitiful Academics are able to cast away or to blind their own perceptions, although this is the thing that they have striven with all their zeal to do.

6. How shameful is this! that a man having received from Nature measures and canons for the recognition of truth, should study not to add to them and perfect them where they are wanting, but the very contrary of this; if there be anything that may lead us to the knowledge of the truth, they strive to abolish and destroy it.

7. What sayest thou, philosopher? religion and holiness, what dost thou take them for?[2]

—— "If thou wilt, I shall prove that they are good."

So be it; prove it then, in order that our citizens

may be converted and honour the Divinity, and be no longer neglectful of the greatest things.

―――" Now hast thou received the proofs ? "

I have, and am thankful therefor.

8. ―――" Now since thou art exceedingly well pleased with these things, hear the contrary: There are no Gods, or if there be, they have no care for men, nor have we any communion with them; and this religion and holiness, whereof the multitude babble, is the lying of impostors and sophists, or of legislators, by Zeus! for the frighting and restraining of evil-doers."

Well said, philosopher! the citizens shall have much profit of thee! thou hast already brought back all our youths to the contempt of sacred things.

――― " What now ? are these doctrines not pleasing to thee ? Learn, then, that Righteousness is nothing, that Reverence is folly, that a father is nothing, a son nothing."

Well said, philosopher! proceed, persuade the young, that we may multiply the number of those who believe and speak with thee. From these teachings have grown our well-governed States, from these did Sparta spring, and these beliefs, by his laws and discipline, did Lycurgus plant among his people:— That slavery is no more base than honourable, nor to be free men more honourable than base. Through these opinions died those who fell at Thermopylæ, and through what others did the Athenians forsake their city ?[3]

9. Then those who speak such things marry, and beget children, and take part in public affairs, and

make themselves priests and augurs—of what? Of beings that do not exist! and they question the Pythian oracle that they may learn falsehoods; and they declare the oracles to others. O monstrous impudence and imposture!

---

## CHAPTER IV.

### ON SLAVERY.

1. A CERTAIN man having inquired how one may make his meals in a manner pleasing to the Gods, If he do it uprightly, said Epictetus, and considerately, and equably, and temperately, and orderly, shall it not also be thus pleasing to the Gods? But when you ask for hot water, and the boy does not hear, or, hearing, brings it only luke-warm; or if he is not even to be found in the house, then is it not pleasing to the Gods if you refrain from indignation, and do not burst with passion? *How shall one endure such fellows?* Wretch, wilt thou not bear with thine own brother, who is of the progeny of Zeus, like a son sprung of the same seed as thyself, and of the same heavenly descent, but thou must straightway make thyself a tyrant, for the place of command in which thou art set? Wilt thou not remember who thou art, and whom thou rulest—that they are kinsmen, brethren by nature, the progeny of Zeus? *But I have bought them, and they have not bought me!* Seest thou, then,

whither thou art looking—towards the earth, towards the pit of perdition, towards these miserable laws of dead men? but towards the laws of the Gods thou dost not look.

2. That which thou wouldst not suffer thyself, seek not to lay upon others. Thou wouldst not be a slave —look to it, that others be not slaves to thee. For if thou endure to have slaves, it seems that thou thyself art first of all a slave. For virtue hath no communion with vice nor freedom with slavery.

3. As one who is in health would not choose to be served by the sick, nor that those dwelling with him should be sick, so neither would one that is free bear to be served by slaves, or that those living with him should be slaves.[1]

## CHAPTER V.

### TO THE ADMINISTRATOR OF THE FREE CITIES, WHO WAS AN EPICUREAN.

1. THE Administrator[1] having visited him (and this man was an Epicurean), It is proper, said Epictetus, that ignorant people like us should inquire of you that are philosophers (as men who come into a strange city make inquiry of the citizens and those familiar with the place) what is the chief thing in the world, to the end that, having learned it, we may go in search of it, and behold it, as men do with objects in the cities.

2. Now, that there are three things with which man is concerned—soul, and body, and the outer world—scarce anyone will deny. It remaineth, then, for men like ye to answer which is the chief of these things? What shall we declare to men? Is it the flesh? And was it for this that Maximus sent forth his son, and sailed with him through the tempest as far as Cassiope,² for somewhat that he should feel in the flesh?

3. But the Epicurean denying this, and saying, *God forbid*, Epictetus said:

Is it not fit, then, that we should be zealous about that, the chief thing?

——" Of all things most fit."

What, then, have we greater than the flesh?

——" The soul," he said.

And the good of the chief thing, is it greater than the good of the lower thing?

——" The good of the chief thing is greater."

And the good things of the soul, are they in the power of the Will, or beyond the Will?

——" They are in the power of the Will."

The pleasure of the soul, then, is within the power of the Will?

He assented.

And this pleasure itself, whence may it arise? From itself? But this is inconceivable; for we must suppose some original substance of the Good, whereof the soul doth make us sensible when we light upon it.

This, too, he admitted.

Wherein, then, are we sensible of this spiritual

pleasure? for if it be in spiritual things, the nature of the Good is discovered. For the Good cannot be something different from the thing that justly delights us; nor, if the original thing be not good, can aught be good that proceeds from it; for, in order that the thing proceeding may be good, the original thing must be good also. But this ye would never say, if ye had your wits, for so ye would speak things that agree not with Epicurus and the rest of your opinions. It remains, then, that we are conscious in bodily things of this pleasure of the soul, and again, that these are the original things and the very substance of the Good.[3]

4. Wherefore Maximus did foolishly if he made his voyage for the sake of anything else than the flesh; that is, than the chief thing. And any man doth foolishly who restraineth himself from others' good, if he be a judge, and able to take them. But, if you please, let us regard this only, how it may be done secretly and safely, and so that none may know it. For neither does Epicurus himself declare stealing to be bad, but only to be caught stealing; and because it is impossible to be certain of no discovery, therefore he saith, *Ye shall not steal.* But I say that if we steal with skill and discretion, we shall not be caught. And, moreover, if we have powerful friends among men and women at Rome, and the Greeks are feeble, no one will dare to go thither on this score. Why do you refrain from your own good? This is foolish— this is absurd. But not even if you tell me you do refrain will I believe you. For, as it is impossible to

assent to anything that appeareth to be a falsehood, or to turn away from what appeareth to be true, even so it is impossible to withhold oneself from anything that appeareth to be good. But riches are a good, and, at all events, the most potent means of pleasure. Wherefore, then, not compass them? And why not corrupt our neighbour's wife, if we may do it secretly? and also, if the husband talk nonsense about it, let us fling him out! If you will be a true and perfect philosopher, and obedient to your own doctrines, thus must you do; but if you do not, you differ no whit from us that are called Stoics. For truly we ourselves say one thing and do another; we speak fair and honest things, and do vile ones. But the opposite distemper will be thine—a vile creed and honourable deeds.

5. And you think, God help you! of a city of Epicureans? *I do not marry. Nor I; for it is not right to marry, nor beget children, nor take part in public affairs.* What will come to pass then? Whence shall we have citizens? who shall educate them? who shall be the overseer of youth?[4] who the director of gymnastics? and how shall the youth be trained up? as the Lacedæmonians? or as the Athenians? Take me a youth, and bring him up after these doctrines of thine! Evil are they, subversive of States, mischievous to households, unbecoming to women. Abandon them, man! Thou dwellest in a chief city; it is thy part to rule, to judge righteously, to refrain from other men's goods; nor must any woman seem beautiful to thee save thine own wife, nor vessel of gold or silver. Seek for

doctrines in harmony with these words, from which setting out thou mayest with gladness abandon things so potent to attract and overcome. But if beside the seduction of these things we have sought out some philosophy like this that pushes us towards them, and confirms us in them, what shall come of it ?

6. In the graver's work, which is the chief thing? the silver or the art? The substance of the hand is flesh, but the main things are the works of the hand. The obligations, therefore, are also three—those that concern us, firstly, in that we are; and secondly, as we are; and thirdly, the main things themselves. And thus in man, too, it is not meet to value the material, this flesh, but the main things. What are these? To take part in public affairs, to marry, to beget children, to fear God, to care for parents, and, in general, to pursue, to avoid, to desire, to dislike, as each of these things should be done, as Nature made us to do. And how made she us? To be free, generous, pious. For what other creature blushes? what other is capable of the sense of shame?

7. And to these things let Pleasure be subject as a minister, a servant, that she may summon forth our ardour, and that she also may aid in works that are according to Nature.[5]

8. ——" But I am a wealthy man, and have no need of aught."

Why, then, dost thou profess philosophy? Thy vessels of gold and vessels of silver are enough for thee; what need hast thou of doctrines?

——" But I am also a judge of the Greeks!"

## TO THE ADMINISTRATOR.

Dost thou know how to judge—who made thee know?

——"Cæsar wrote me a commission."

Let him write thee a commission to be a judge of music, and what help will it be to thee? And how didst thou become a judge? by kissing of what man's hand? Was it that of Symphorus or Numenius? Before whose bed-chamber didst thou sleep? To whom didst thou send gifts? Dost thou not perceive, then, that to be a judge is worth just as much as Numenius is worth?

——"But I can cast into prison whom I will."

As if he were a stone.

——"But I can flog any man I will."

As if he were an ass. This is no government of men. Rule us as reasoning beings; show us what is for our good, and we shall follow it; show us what is for our ill, and we shall turn away from it; make us emulators of thyself, as Socrates made his disciples. He, indeed, was one that governed men as men, who made them subject unto him in their pursuit and their avoidance, their desire and dislike. *Do this, do not this, or I will cast thee into prison.* This is not the rule of reasoning beings. But, *As Zeus hath ordered, so do thou act; but if thou dost not, thou shalt suffer loss and hurt.* What hurt? *None other than this—not to have done what it behoved thee to do. Thou shalt lose faith, piety, decency—look for no greater injuries than these.*

## CHAPTER VI.

### ON STATECRAFT.

1. Not with the stones of Euboea and Sparta let the structure of your city walls be variegated; but let the discipline and teaching that comes from Greece penetrate with order the minds of citizens and statesmen. *For with the thoughts of men are cities well established, and not with wood and stone.*

2. If thou wouldst have a household well established, then follow the example of the Spartan Lycurgus. For even as he did not fence the city with walls, but fortified the inhabitants with virtue, and so preserved the city free for ever, thus do thou not surround thyself with a great court and set up lofty towers, but confirm the dwellers in the house with goodwill, and faith, and friendliness, and no harmful thing shall enter; no, not if the whole army of evil were arrayed against it.

3. Which of us will not admire Lycurgus, the Lacedæmonian? For having lost an eye at the hands of one of the citizens, and having received the young man from the people that he should punish him as he would, he refrained from this; but having taught him and proved him to be a good man, he brought him into the theatre. And when the Lacedæmonians marvelled, *I received this man from you,* he said, *insolent and violent; I give him back to you mild and civil.*

## CHAPTER VII.

### ON FRIENDSHIP.

1. WHEREINSOEVER a man is zealous, this, it is fair to suppose, he loveth. Are men, then, zealous for evil things? Never.[1] Or, perchance, for things which do not concern them? Nor for them either. It remaineth, then, that they are zealous about good things only; and that if they are zealous about them, they also love them. Whosoever, then, hath understanding of good things, the same would know how to love. But he who is not able to distinguish good things from evil, and things that are neither from both, how could this man yet be capable of loving? To love, then, is a quality of the wise alone.

2. *And how is this*, saith one, *for I am foolish, and none the less do I love my child.* By the Gods! I wonder, then, how you have begun by confessing yourself to be foolish. For wherein do you lack? Do you not use your senses? do you not judge of appearances? do you not bring to the body the nourishment it needeth, and the covering and habitation? Wherefore, then, confess yourself to be a fool? Because, forsooth, you are often perplexed by appearances, and troubled, and you are vanquished by their plausibility; and you take the same things to be now good, and now evil, and then indifferent; and, in a word, you grieve and fear and envy, and are

troubled, and changed—for these things you confess yourself a fool.

3. But do you never change in love? But is it wealth, and pleasure, and, in short, things alone that you sometimes take to be good and sometimes evil? and do you not take the same men to be now good, now evil? and sometimes you are friendly disposed towards them, and sometimes hostile? and sometimes you praise them, and sometimes you blame?

——" Yea, even so I do."

What then? a man who hath been deceived about another, is he, think you, his friend?

——" Assuredly not."

And one who hath taken a friend out of a humour for change, hath he good-will towards him?

——" Nor he either."

And he who now reviles another, and afterwards reveres him?

——" Nor he."

What then? Sawest thou never the whelps of a dog, how they fawn and sport with each other, that you would say nothing can be more loving? But to know what friendship is, fling a piece of flesh among them, and thou shalt learn. And cast between thee and thy child a scrap of land, and thou shalt learn how the child will quickly wish to bury thee, and thou wilt pray that he may die. And then thou wilt say, *What a child have I nourished! this long time he is burying me!* Throw a handsome girl between you, and the old man will love her, and the young too;[2] and if it be glory, or some risk to run, it will be on

## ON FRIENDSHIP.

the same fashion. You will speak the words of the father of Admetus[3]:—

> "Day gladdens thee; think'st thou it glads not me?
> Thou lovest light; think'st thou I love the dark?"

Think you this man did not love his own child when it was little? nor was in agony if it had a fever? nor said many a time, *Would that I had the fever rather than he!* Then when the trial cometh and is near at hand, lo, what words they utter! And Eteocles and Polyneices,[4] were they not children of the same mother and the same father? were they not brought up together, did they not live together, drink together, sleep together, and often kiss one another? So that anyone who saw them, I think, would have laughed at the philosophers, for the things they say perversely about friendship. But when royalty, like a piece of flesh, hath fallen between them, hear what things they speak:—

> *Pol.* Where wilt thou stand before the towers?
> *Et.* Wherefore seekest thou to know?
> *Pol.* There I too would stand and slay thee.
> *Et.* Thou hast spoken my desire.

4. For universally, be not deceived, nothing is so dear to any creature as its own profit. Whatsoever may seem to hinder this, be it father or child or friend or lover, this he will hate and abuse and curse. For Nature hath never so made anything as to love aught but its own profit: this is father and brother and kin and country and God. When, then, the Gods appear to hinder us in this, we revile even them, and

overthrow their images and burn their temples; as Alexander, when his friend died, commanded to burn the temples of Esculapius.

5. Therefore, if a man place in the same thing both profit and holiness, and the beautiful and fatherland, and parents and friends, all these things shall be saved; but if he place profit in one thing, and friends and fatherland and kinsfolk, yea, and righteousness itself some other where, all these things shall perish, for profit shall outweigh them. For where the I and the Mine are, thither, of necessity, inclineth every living thing: if in the flesh, then the supremacy is there; if in the Will, it is there; if in outward things, it is there. If, then, mine I is where my Will is, thus only shall I be the friend I should be, or the son or the father. For my profit then will be to cherish faith and piety and forbearance and continence and helpfulness; and to guard the bonds of relation. But if I set Myself in one place and Virtue some otherwhere, then the word of Epicurus waxeth strong, which declareth that there is no Virtue, or, at least, that Virtue is but conceit.

6. Through this ignorance did Athenians and Lacedæmonians quarrel with each other, and Thebans with both of them, and the Great King with Hellas, and Macedonians with both of them, and even now Romans with Getæ; and through this yet earlier the wars of Ilion arose. Paris was the guest of Menelaus; and if anyone had seen how friendly-minded towards each other they were, he would have disbelieved anyone who said they were not friends.

But a morsel was flung between them—a fair woman, and about her there was war. And now when you see friends or brothers that seem to be of one mind, argue nothing from this concerning their friendship; nay, not if they swear it, not if they declare that they cannot be parted from each other. For in the ruling faculty of a worthless man there is no faith; it is unstable, unaccountable, victim of one appearance after another. But try them, not, as others do, if they were born of the same parents and nurtured together, and under the same tutor; but by this alone, wherein they place their profit, whether in outward things or in the will. If in outward things, call them no more friends than faithful or steadfast or bold or free; yea, nor even men, if you had sense. For that opinion hath nothing of humanity that makes men bite each other, and revile each other, and haunt the wildernesses, or the public places, like the mountains,[5] and in the courts of justice to show forth the character of thieves; nor that which makes men drunkards and adulterers and corruptors, nor whatever other ills men work against each other through this one and only opinion, that They and Theirs lie in matters beyond the Will. But if you hear, in sooth, that these men hold the Good to be there only where the Will is, where the right use of appearances is, then be not busy to inquire if they are father and son, or brothers, or have long time companied with each other as comrades; but, knowing this one thing alone, argue confidently that they are friends, even as they are faithful and upright. For where else is friendship than where faith is, where piety is, where there is an interchange of virtue, and none of other things than that?

7. *But such a one hath shown kindness to me so long, and is he not my friend?* Slave, whence knowest thou if he did not show thee kindness as he wipes his shoes or tends his beast? Whence knowest thou if, when thy use is at an end as a vessel, he will not cast thee away like a broken plate? *But she is my wife, and we have lived together so long?* And how long lived Eriphyle with Amphiaraus, and was the mother, yea, of many children? But a necklace came between them.[6] But what is a necklace? It is the opinion men have concerning such things. That was the wild beast nature, that was the sundering of love, that which would not allow the woman to be a wife, or the mother a mother. And of you, whosoever hath longed either to be a friend himself or to win some other for a friend, let him cut out these opinions, let him hate them and drive them from his soul.

8. And thus he will not revile himself, nor be at strife with himself, nor be variable, nor torment himself. And to another, if it be one like himself, he will be altogether as to himself, but with one unlike he will be forbearing and gentle and mild, ready to forgive him as an ignorant man, as one who is astray about the greatest things; but harsh to no man, being well-assured of that dogma of Plato, that no soul is willingly deprived of the truth.

9. But otherwise ye may do all things whatsoever, even as friends are wont to do, and drink together,

and dwell together, and voyage together, and be born from the same parents, for so are snakes; but friends, they are not, nor are ye, so long as ye hold these accursed doctrines of wild beasts.

## CHAPTER VIII.

### TIME AND CHANGE.

1. LET not another's vice be thy evil. For thou wast not born to be abject with others, or unfortunate with others, but to prosper with them. But if anyone is unfortunate, remember that it is of his own doing. For God hath made all men to be happy, and of good estate. For this end hath he granted means and occasions, giving some things to each man as his own concern, and some things as alien; and the things that are hindered and subject to compulsion and loss are not his own concern, and those that are unhindered are; and the substance of Good and of Evil, as it were worthy of him that careth for us and doth protect us as a father, he hath placed among our own concerns.

2. —— "But I have parted from such a one, and he is grieved."

For why did he deem things alien to be his own concern? Why, when he rejoiced to see thee did he not reason that thou wert mortal, and apt to travel to another land? Therefore doth he pay the penalty of his own folly. But thou, for what cause or reason dost thou bewail thyself? Hast thou also given no thought to these things; but like silly women consorted with all that pleased thee as though thou shouldst consort with them forever, places and persons and pastimes? and now thou sittest weeping, because thou canst see the same persons and frequent the same places no longer. This, truly, is what thou art fit for, to be more wretched than crows and ravens that can fly whithersoever they please, and change their nests, and pass across the seas, nor ever lament nor yearn for what they have left.

——"Yea, but they are thus because they are creatures without reason."

To us, then, was Reason given by the Gods for our misfortune and misery? that we should be wretched and sorrowful forever? Let all men be immortal, forsooth, and no man migrate to another land, nor let us ourselves ever migrate, but remain rooted to one spot like plants; and if one of our companions go, let us sit down and weep, and if he return, dance and clap hands like children!

3. Shall we not now at last wean ourselves, and remember what we heard from the philosophers? if, indeed, we did not listen to them as a wizard's incantation. For they said that the universe is one Polity, and one is the substance out of which it is made, and there must, of necessity, be a certain cycle, and some things must give place to others, some dissolving away, and others coming into being, some abiding in one place, and others being in motion. But all things are

full of love, first of the Gods, then of men, that are by nature made to have affection towards each other ; and it must needs be that some dwell with each other, and some are separated, rejoicing in those who are with them, and not distressed for those who go away. And man, they said, is magnanimous by nature, and contemneth all things beyond the Will; and hath also this quality, not to be rooted to one spot, nor grown into the earth, but able to go from place to place, sometimes urged by divers needs, sometimes for the sake of what he shall see.

4. And such was the case with Ulysses :—

"The cities of many peoples and minds of men he knew."
—*Od.* i. 3.

And yet earlier with Hercules, who went about the whole earth—

"All disorders of men and orderly rule to see,"
—*Od.* xvii. 487.

casting out and purging the one, and bringing in the other in its place. And how many friends, think you, had he in Thebes ? how many in Argos ? how many in Athens ? and how many did he gain in his journeyings ? And he took a wife, too, when it seemed to him due time, and begat children, and left them behind him, not with lamentations or regrets, nor leaving them as orphans ; for he knew that no man is an orphan, but that there is an Eternal Father who careth continually for all. For not of report alone had he heard that Zeus is the Father of men, whom also he thought to be his own father, and called Him so, and all that he did, he did looking unto Him. And thus it was that he was able to live happily in every place.

5. For never can happiness and the longing for what is not exist together. For Happiness must have all its will. It is like unto one that hath eaten and is filled; thirst will not sort with it, nor hunger. *But Ulysses longed for his wife, and lamented as he sat on the rock.*[1] And do you, then, follow Homer and his stories in everything? Or if he did in truth lament, what else was he than an unfortunate man? And what good man is unfortunate? Verily, the Whole is ill-governed if Zeus taketh no care of his own citizens, that they like himself may be happy; but these things it is not lawful nor pious even to think of. But Ulysses, if indeed he lamented and complained, was not a good man. For what good man is there that knoweth not who he is? and who knoweth this who forgets that things which come into existence also perish, and that no two human beings dwell together for ever? To aim, then, at things which are impossible is a contemptible and foolish thing; it is the part of a stranger and alien in God's world who fights against God in the one way he can—by his own opinions.

6. *But my mother laments if she sees me not.* And wherefore hath she never learned these teachings? Yet, I say not that it is no concern of ours to prevent her grieving; but that we should not absolutely, and without exception, desire what is not our own. And the grief of another is another's, and my grief is mine

## TIME AND CHANGE.

own. I will, therefore, absolutely end mine own grief, for this I can; and that of another according to my means, but this I will not attempt absolutely. For otherwise I shall be fighting with God. I shall be opposing and resisting him in the government of the Whole; and of this strife against God, this obstinacy, not only my children's children, but I myself, too, shall pay the penalty by day and night; for I shall leap from my bed at visions of the night, confounded, trembling at every news, having my peace at the mercy of letters of other persons. *A messenger hath come from Rome; God grant it be no evil.* But what evil can come upon thee there, where thou art not? *There is a message from Greece; God grant it be no evil.* And thus to thee every place may be a source of misfortune. Is it not enough for thee to be unfortunate where thou art, and not also across the sea, and by writings? Is this the security of thine affairs? *But what if my friends which are abroad die there?* What else than that creatures destined to die have died? And how dost thou desire to live to old age, and never to see the death of any whom thou lovest? Knowest thou not that in a great length of time many and various things must chance; that a fever shall overthrow one, and a robber another, and a tyrant another? Such is our environment, such our companions; cold and heat, and improper ways of living, and journeyings, and voyagings, and winds, and various circumstances will destroy one man, and exile another, and cast another into an embassy, and another into a campaign. Sit down, then, terrified at all these things; grieve and fail, and be unfortunate; depend on others, and that not on one or two, but myriads upon myriads.

7. Is this what you heard, is this what you learned from the philosophers? Know you not that our business here is a warfare? and one must watch, and one go out as a spy, and one must fight? All cannot be the same thing, nor would it be better if they were. But you neglect to do the bidding of the commander, and complain when he hath laid somewhat rougher than common upon you; and you mark not what, so far as in you lies, you are making the army to become, so that if all copy you, none will dig a trench, none will cast up a rampart, none will watch, none will run any risk, but each will appear worthless for warfare. Again, in a ship, if you go for a sailor, take up one place, and never budge from it; and if you are wanted to go aloft, refuse; or to run upon the prow, refuse; and what captain will have patience with you? Will he not cast you out like some useless thing, nothing else than a hindrance and bad example to the other sailors?

8. And thus here also: the life of every man is a sort of warfare, and a long one, and full of divers chances. And it behoveth a man to play a soldier's part, and do all at the nod of his commander; yea, and if it be possible, to divine what he intendeth. For that commander is not such a one as this, neither in power nor in exaltation of character. You are set in a great office, and in no mean place, but are a Senator for ever. Know you not that such a one can

attend but little to his household, but he must be oftentimes abroad, ruling or being ruled, or fulfilling some office, or serving in the field, or judging? And will you, then, desire to be fixed and rooted like a plant in the same place? *For it is pleasant.* Who denies it? But so is a dainty pleasant, and a fair woman is pleasant. How otherwise are those wont to speak who make pleasure their end? See you not what kind of men they are whose words you utter? They are the words of Epicureans and profligates. And doing the works of these men, and holding their doctrines, wilt thou speak to us with the speech of Zeno and Socrates?

9. Will you not fling away from you as far as you can these alien sentiments wherewith you adorn yourself, which beseem you not at all? What other desire have such men than to sleep their fill unhindered, and when they have risen, to yawn for languor, and wash their face, and write and read whatever pleaseth them; then have some trivial talk, and be praised by their friends, whatever they say; then go forth to walk about, and having done this a little, go to the baths; then eat; then retire to rest— such a rest as is the wont of such men, and why need we say what, for it is easily guessed? Come, tell me, then, thine own way of life, such as thou desirest, O thou votary of the truth, and of Socrates and Diogenes! What wilt thou do in Athens? these very things, or others? Why then, dost declare thyself a Stoic? Are not they sorely punished which falsely pretend to be Roman citizens; and should those go

free who falsely pretend to so great and reverend a calling and name? or let this indeed be impossible; but this is the law, divine and mighty, and not to be escaped, that layeth the greatest punishments on the greatest sinners. For what saith this law? He who pretendeth to things that are not his own, let him be a cheat and braggart; he that is disobedient to the divine government, let him be an abject, a slave, let him grieve and envy and pity [2]—in a word, let him be misfortunate, and mourn.

10. ——"And now will you have me attend upon such a one, and hang about his doors?"

If Reason demand it, for the sake of country, of kinsmen, of mankind, wherefore shouldst thou not go? Thou art not ashamed to go to the doors of a cobbler when thou art in want of shoes, nor to those of a gardener for lettuces; and why to those of a rich man when thou art in need of some like thing?

——"Yea, but I have no awe of the cobbler."

Then have none of the rich.

——"Nor will I flatter the gardener."

And do not flatter the rich.

——"How, then, shall I gain what I want?"

Did I say to thee, *Go, for the sake of gaining it;* or did I not only say, *Go, that thou mayest do what it beseems thee to do.*

——"And why, then, should I yet go?"

That thou mayest have gone; that thou mayest have played the part of a citizen, of a brother, of a friend. And, for the rest, remember that the shoemaker, the vegetable-seller, to whom thou didst go, hath nothing great or exalted to give, even though he sell it dear. Thy aim was lettuces; they are worth an obol, they are not worth a talent. And so it is here. Is the matter worth going to the rich man's door for? So be it; I will go. Is it worth speaking to him about? So be it; I will speak. But must I also kiss his hand, and fawn upon him with praise? Out upon it! that is a talent's worth. It is no profit to me, nor to the State, nor to my friends, that they should lose a good citizen and friend.

11. ——"How, then, shall I become of an affectionate disposition?"

In having a generous and happy one. For Reason doth never decree that a man must be abject, or lament, or depend on another, or blame God or man. And thus be thou affectionate, as one who will keep this faith. But if through this affection, or what happens to be so called by thee, thou art like to prove a miserable slave, then it shall not profit thee to be affectionate. And what hinders us to love as though we loved a mortal, or one who may depart to other lands? Did Socrates not love his children? Yea, but as a free man; as one who remembered that he must first love the Gods. And, therefore, he never did transgress anything that it becomes a good man to observe, neither in his defence, nor in fixing his punishment, nor beforetime when he was of the Council, nor when he was serving in the field. But we are well supplied with every excuse for baseness; some through children, some through mothers, some through brothers. But it behoveth no man to be unhappy through any person, but happy through all, and most of all through God, which hath framed us to that end.

12. And, for the rest, in all things which are delightful to thee, set before thyself the appearances that oppose them. What harm is it, while kissing thy child to whisper, *To-morrow thou shalt die;* and likewise with thy friend, *To-morrow thou shalt depart, either thou or I, and we shall see each other no more?*

——" But these are words of ill-omen."

And so are some incantations, but in that they are useful I regard not this; only let them be of use. But dost thou call anything of ill-omen, save only that which betokeneth some evil? Cowardice is a word of ill-omen, and baseness and grief and mourning and shamelessness, these words are of ill-omen. And not even them must we dread to speak, if so we may defend ourselves against the things. But wilt thou say that any word is of ill-omen that betokeneth some natural thing? Say that it is of ill-omen to speak of the reaping of ears of corn, for it betokeneth the destruction of the ears—but not of the universe. Say that the falling of the leaves is of ill-omen, and the dried fig coming in the place of the green, and raisins in the place of grapes. For all these things are changes from the former estate to another; no destruction, but a certain appointed order and disposition. Here is parting for foreign lands, and a little change. Here is death—a greater change, not from that which now is to that which is not, but to that which is not now.

## CHAPTER IX.

### ON SOLITUDE.

1. SOLITUDE is the state of one who is helpless. For he who is alone is not therefore solitary; even as he who is in a great company is not therefore not solitary. When, therefore, we have lost a brother or a son or a friend on whom we were wont to rest, we say that we are left solitary, and oftentimes we say it in Rome, with such a crowd meeting us and so many dwelling about us, and, it may be, having a multitude of slaves. For the solitary man, in his conception, meaneth to be thought helpless, and laid open to those who wish him harm. Therefore when we are on a journey we then, above all, say that we are solitary when we are fallen among thieves; for that which taketh away solitude is not the sight of a man, but of a faithful and pious and serviceable man. For if to be solitary it sufficeth to be alone, then say that Zeus is solitary in the conflagration,[1] and bewails himself. *Woe is me! I have neither Hera nor Athene nor Apollo*, nor, in short, either brother or son or descendant or kinsman. And so some say he doth when alone in the conflagration. For they comprehend not the life of a man who is alone, setting out from a certain natural principle, that we are by nature social, and inclined to love each other, and pleased to be in the company of other men. But none the less is it needful that one find the means to this also, to

be able to suffice to himself, and to be his own companion. For as Zeus is his own companion, and is content with himself, and considereth his own government, what it is, and is occupied in designs worthy of himself; thus should we be able to converse with ourselves, and feel no need of others, nor want means to pass the time; but to observe the divine government, and the relation of ourselves with other things; to consider how we stood formerly towards the events that befall us, and how we stand now; what things they are that still afflict us; how these, too, may be healed, how removed; and if aught should need perfecting, to perfect it according to the reason of the case.

2. Ye see now, how that Cæsar seemeth to have given us a great peace; how there are no longer wars nor battles nor bands of robbers nor of pirates, but a man may travel at every season, and sail from east to west. But can he give us peace from fever? or from shipwreck? or from fire? or earthquake? or lightning? aye, or from love? *He cannot.* Or from grief? *He cannot.* Or from envy? *He cannot.* Briefly, then, he cannot secure us from any of such things. But the word of the philosophers doth promise us peace even from these things. And what saith it? *If ye will hearken unto me, O men, wheresoever ye be, whatsoever ye do, ye shall not grieve, ye shall not be wroth, ye shall not be compelled or hindered, but ye shall live untroubled and free from every ill.* Whosoever hath this peace, which Cæsar never proclaimed (for how could he proclaim it?), but which God

proclaimed through his word, shall he not suffice to himself when he may be alone ? for he beholdeth and considereth, *Now can no evil happen to me; for me there is no robber, no earthquake; all things are full of peace, full of calm; for me no way, no city, no assembly, no neighbour, no associate hath any hurt.* He is supplied by one, whose part that is, with food, by another with raiment, by another with senses, by another with natural conceptions. And when it may be that the necessary things are no longer supplied, that is the signal for retreat : the door is opened, and God saith to thee, *Depart.*

———" Whither ? "

To nothing dreadful, but to the place from whence thou camest—to things friendly and akin to thee, to the elements of Being. Whatever in thee was fire shall go to fire; of earth, to earth; of air, to air; of water, to water;[2] no Hades, nor Acheron, nor Coeytus, nor Phlegethon, but all things are full of Gods and Powers.[3] Whoso hath these things to think on, and seeth the sun and the moon and the stars, and rejoiceth in the earth and the sea, he is no more solitary than he is helpless.

———" What, then, if one come and find me alone and slay me ? "

Fool ! not thee, but thy wretched body.

3. Thou art a little soul bearing up a corpse.

4. What solitude, then, is there any longer, what lack ? Why do we make ourselves worse than children, which, when they are left alone, what do they ?—they take shells and sand and build up

somewhat, and then throw it down, and again build up something else, and so they never lack pastime. And shall I, if ye sail away from me, sit down and weep for that I am left alone and solitary? Shall I have no shells nor sand? But children do these things through their folly, and we through our wisdom are made unhappy.

## CHAPTER X.

### AGAINST THE CONTENTIOUS AND REVENGEFUL.

1. To suppose that we shall become contemptible in the eyes of others unless in some way we inflict an injury on those who first shewed hostility to us, is the character of most ignoble and thoughtless men. For thus we say, that a man is to be despised according to his inability to do hurt; but much rather is he to be despised according to his inability to do good.

2. The wise and good man neither strives with any himself, nor in the measure of his power will he allow another to strive. And in this, as in all other things, the life of Socrates is set before us as an example; who did not only himself fly all contention, but also forbade it to others. See in Xenophon's *Symposium* how many quarrels he ended; and, again, how he bore with Thrasymachus, and how with Polus and with Callicles; and how he endured his wife, and how his son, which opposed him with sophistical arguments.

## AGAINST THE CONTENTIOUS.

For he remembered very well that no man can command the ruling faculty of another.

3. How then, is there yet any place for contention in one so minded? For what event can amaze him? what appear strange to him? Doth he not look for even worse and more grievous things at the hands of evil men than do befall him? Doth he not count everything for gain which is short of the extreme of injury? Hath such a one reviled thee? Much thanks to him that he did not strike thee. *But he did also strike me.* Much thanks that he did not wound thee. *But he did also wound me.* Much thanks that he did not slay thee. For when did he learn, or from whom, that he was a tame animal, and affectionate to others, and that to the wrongdoer the wrongdoing itself is a heavy injury? For since he hath not learned these things, nor believes them, wherefore should he not follow that which appears to be his advantage? Thy neighbour hath flung stones? Hast thou, then, sinned in aught? But he has broken things in the house? And art thou a household vessel? Nay—but a Will.

4. What, then, hath been given thee for this occasion? To a wolf it were given to bite—to fling more stones. But if thou seek what is becoming for a man, look into thy stores, see what faculties thou hast come here furnished withal. Hast thou the nature of a wild beast? the temper of revenge?

5. When is a horse in wretched case? When he is bereaved of his natural faculties; not when he cannot crow, but when he cannot run. When is a dog?

Not when he cannot fly, but when he cannot track. Is not a man, then, also thus wretched, not when he cannot strangle lions or embrace statues[1]—for to this he came endowed with no faculties by Nature—but when he hath lost his honesty, his faithfulness? Surely we should meet together and lament over such a man; so great are the evils into which he hath fallen. Not, indeed, that we should lament for his birth, or for his death, but in that while yet living he hath suffered the loss of his own true possessions. I speak not of his paternal inheritance, not of his land, or his house, or his inn, or his slaves (for not one of these things is the true possession of a man, but all are alien, servile, subject, given now to some, now to others, by those that can command them); but of his human qualities, the stamps of his spirit wherewith he came into the world. Even such we seek for also on coins, and if we find them we approve the coins; if not, we cast them away. What is the stamp of this sestertius? *The stamp of Trajan.* Then give it me. *The stamp of Nero.*[2] Fling it away—it will not pass, it is bad. And so here too. What is the stamp of his mind? He is gentle, social, forbearing, affectionate. Come, then, I receive him, I admit him to citizenship, I receive him as a neighbour, a fellow-traveller. See to it only that he have not Nero's stamp. Is he wrathful, revengeful, complaining? Doth he, when it may seem good to him, break the heads of all who stand in his way? Why, then, did'st thou say he was a man? Shall everything be judged by the bare form? If so, then say that a wax apple is a real apple, and that it has the smell and taste of an apple. But the outward shape doth not suffice, nor are eyes and nose enough to make a man, but he is a man only if he have a man's mind. Here is one that will not hear reason, that will not submit when he is confuted—he is an ass. In another, reverence hath died—he is worthless, anything rather than a man. This one seeketh whom he may meet and kick or bite—so that he is not even a sheep or an ass, but some kind of savage beast.

6. But this is the nature of every creature, to pursue the Good and fly the Evil; and to hold every man an enemy and a plotter for our woe, were it even a brother, or son, or father, who takes away from us the one, or brings us into the other. For nothing is nearer or dearer to us than the Good. It remains, therefore, if outward things be good and evil, that a father is no longer the friend of his sons, nor the brother of his brother, but every place is full of enemies and plotters and slanderers. But if the only Good is that the Will should be as it ought to be, and the only Evil as it ought not, where is there then any place for strife, for reviling? For about what things shall we strive? about those that are nothing to us? and with whom? with the ignorant, the unhappy, with men who are deceived concerning the greatest things?

7. Remembering these thing, Socrates managed his own household, enduring a most shrewish wife and an undutiful son. For these doctrines make love in a household, and concord in a State, peace among nations, and gratitude towards God, with boldness in

every place, as of one who hath to do with things alien to him, and of no estimation. And we are the men to write and read these things, and to applaud them when they are delivered to us, but to the belief of them we have not even come near. And therefore that saying concerning the Lacedæmonians,

"Lions at home, but in Ephesus foxes,"[3]

will fit us too—lions in the school and foxes without.

END OF BOOK III.

# BOOK IV.

## CHAPTER I.

### OF RELIGION.

1. OF religion towards the Gods, know that the chief element is to have right opinions concerning them, as existing and governing the whole in fair order and justice; and then to set thyself to obey them, and to yield to them in each event, and submit to it willingly, as accomplished under the highest counsels. For so shalt thou never blame the Gods, nor accuse them, as being neglectful of thee.

2. But this may come to pass in no other way than by placing Good and Evil in the things that are in our own power, and withdrawing them from those that are not; for if thou take any of these things to be good or evil, then when thou shalt miss thy desire, or fall into what thou desirest not, it is altogether necessary that thou blame and hate those who caused thee to do so.

3. For every living thing was so framed by Nature as to flee and turn from things, and the causes of things, that appear hurtful, and to follow and admire things, and the causes of things, that appear serviceable. For it is impossible that one who thinketh

himself harmed should delight in that seemeth to harm him, even as he cannot delight in the very harm itself.

4. And thus it comes that a father is reviled by his son when he will not give him of the things that appear to be good. And this it was that set Polyneices and Eteocles at war with each other—the opinion, namely, that royalty is a good. And through this the Gods are railed on by the husbandman and the sailor, by the merchant, and men who lose their wives or children. For where advantage is, there also is religion. Thus he who is careful to pursue and avoid as he ought, is careful, at the same time, of religion.

5. But it is fitting also that every man should pour libations and offer sacrifices and first-fruits after the customs of his fathers, purely, and not languidly nor negligently, nor, indeed, scantily, nor yet beyond his means.

## CHAPTER II.

### OF PROVIDENCE.

1. CONCERNING the Gods, there are some who say that a Divine Being does not exist; and others, that it exists indeed, but is idle and uncaring, and hath no forethought for anything; and a third class say that there is such a Being, and he taketh forethought also,

## OF PROVIDENCE.

but only in respect of great and heavenly things, but of nothing that is on the earth; and a fourth class, that he taketh thought of things both in heaven and earth, but only in general, and not of each thing severally. And there is a fifth class, whereof are Odysseus and Socrates, who say, *Nor can I move without thy knowledge.*[1]

2. Before all things, then, it is necessary to investigate each of these opinions, whether it be justly affirmed or no. For if there be no Gods, how can the following of the Gods be an end? And if there are Gods, but such as take no care for anything, then also how can the following of them be truly an end? And how, again, if the Gods both exist and take care for things, yet if there be no communication from them to men, yea, by Zeus, and even to mine own self? The wise and good man, having investigated all these things, will submit his own mind to Him that governeth the Whole, even as good citizens to the laws of their State.

3. But a certain man having inquired how one could be persuaded that every one of his actions is observed by God, Doth it not appear to you, said Epictetus, that all things are united in One?

——" It doth so appear."

What then? Think you not that a sympathy exists between heavenly and earthly things?

——"I do think it."

For how else do plants, as if at the command of God, when he bids them, flower in due season? and shoot forth when he bids them shoot, and bear fruit when he bids them bear? and ripen when he bids them ripen? and again they drop their fruit when he bids them drop it, and shed their leaves when he bids them shed them? and how else at his bidding do they fold themselves together, and remain motionless and at rest? And how else at the waxing and waning of the moon, and the approach and withdrawal of the sun, do we behold such a change and reversal in earthly things? But are the plants and our bodies so bound up in the whole, and have sympathy with it, and are our spirits not much more so? And our souls being thus bound up and in touch with God, seeing, indeed, that they are portions and fragments of him, shall not every movement of them, inasmuch as it is something inward and akin to God, be perceived by him? But you are able to meditate upon the divine government, and upon all divine and all human affairs, and to be affected at the same time in the senses and in the intellect by ten thousand things, and at the same time to assent to some and dissent to others, or suspend your judgment; and you preserve in your mind so many impressions of so many and various things, and being affected by them, you strike upon ideas similar to earlier impressions, and you retain many different arts, and memories of ten thousand things; and shall not God have the power to overlook all things, and be present with all, and have a certain communication with all? But is the sun able to illuminate so great a part of the All, and to leave so little without light,—that part, namely, which is filled with the shadow of the earth—and shall He

## OF PROVIDENCE.

who made the sun, and guideth it in its sphere—a small part of Him beside the Whole—shall He not be capable of perceiving all things?

4. *But I,* saith the man, *cannot take heed of all these things at once.* And who said you could do this? that you had equal powers with God? But, nevertheless, He hath placed at every man's side a Guardian, the Genius of each man,[2] who is charged to watch over him, a Genius that cannot sleep, nor be deceived. To what greater and more watchful guardian could he have committed us? So, when ye have shut the doors, and made darkness in the house, remember never to say that ye are alone; for ye are not alone, but God is there, and your Genius is there; and what need have these of light to mark what ye are doing? To this God it were fitting also that ye should swear an oath, as soldiers do to Cæsar. But those indeed who receive pay swear to prefer the safety of Cæsar before all things; but ye, receiving so many and great things, will ye not swear? or swearing, will ye not abide by it? And what shall ye swear? Never to disobey, never to accuse, never to blame aught that He hath given, never unwillingly to do or suffer any necessary thing. Is this oath like unto that other? The soldiers swear to esteem no other man before Cæsar; ye to esteem yourselves above all.

## CHAPTER III.

#### OF PROVIDENCE.

1. Marvel not if the other animals have all things that are needful for the body without preparation, not alone food and drink, but sleeping places also, and they have no need of shoes, nor bedding, nor raiment, while all these things must needs be added to us. For these creatures exist not for themselves, but for service; it were not expedient that they had been made with need of such additions. For, look you, what a task it were for us to take thought, not for ourselves alone, but also for the sheep and the asses, how they should be clad, how shod, how they should eat, how they should drink! But as soldiers are ready for their commands, shod, and clothed, and accoutred, and it would be a grievous thing if each captain of a thousand must go round and shoe or clothe his thousand; so also hath Nature formed the animals that are made for service, ready equipped, and needing no further care. And thus one little child with a rod will drive the sheep.

2. But now we, neglecting to be grateful, for that we need not attend to the animals equally with ourselves, do accuse God for our own lack. And yet, by Zeus and all the Gods, there is no one thing in the frame of Nature but would give, at least to a reverent and grateful spirit, enough for the perceiving of the Providence of God. And to speak of no great things

## OF PROVIDENCE.

now, consider this alone, how milk is produced from grass, and cheese from milk, and wool from skins. Who is he that hath made these things or planned them? *No one,* sayest thou? O monstrous impudence and dulness!

3. Well, then, let the large works of Nature pass, and let us look only at her by-works. Is there aught more useless than the hairs on the chin? What then? hath she not made such use even of these, that nothing could be comelier? hath she not by them distinguished male from female? Doth not the nature of every man cry aloud even at a distance, *I am a man, thus shalt thou approach me, thus speak to me, look for nothing else; behold the tokens!* And again in women, as Nature hath mingled something of softness in the voice, so she hath taken away the hairs. *Nay,* will you say? *but every creature should have been left undistinguished, and each of us should proclaim, "I am a man?"* But how beautiful is not the token, and becoming, and reverend? how much more beautiful than the cock's comb? how much more becoming than the lion's mane? Wherefore it behoveth us to preserve God's tokens, nor to fling them away, nor to confound, as far as in us lies, the things that distinguish the sexes.

4. Are these the only works of Providence in us?—but what may suffice to rightly praise and tell them? For had we understanding thereof, would any other thing better beseem us, either in company or alone, than to hymn the Divine Being, and laud Him and rehearse His gracious deeds? Should we not, as we dig or plough or eat, sing this hymn to God, *Great is*

*God, who hath given us such instruments whereby we shall till the earth: great is God, who hath given us hands, and swallowing, and the belly; who maketh us to grow without our knowledge, and to breathe while we sleep.* These things it were fitting that every man should sing, and to chant the greatest and divinest hymns for this, that He hath given us the power to observe and consider His works and a Way wherein to walk.[1] What then? since the most of you have become blind, should there not be one to fill this place, and in the name of all to sing this hymn to God? For what else can I do, an old man and lame, than sing hymns to God? If I were a nightingale I would do after the nature of a nightingale; if a swan, after that of a swan. But now I am a reasoning creature, and it behoves me to sing the praise of God: this is my task, and this I do, nor, as long as it is granted me, will I ever abandon this post. And you, too, I summon to join me in the same song.

## CHAPTER IV.

### GOD IN MAN.

1. GOD is beneficial. But the Good is also beneficial. It is likely, then, that where the essence of God is, there also should be the essence of the Good. And what is the essence of God? Flesh? God forbid.

## GOD IN MAN.

A property in land? God forbid. Fame? God forbid. Mind, Intelligence, Right Reason? Even so. Here, then, once for all, seek the essence of the Good. For surely you will in no wise seek it in a plant? *Nay.* Or in any unreasoning creature? *Nay.* If, then, it is sought in a reasoning creature, wherefore continue to seek it anywhere else than in the difference between reasoning and unreasoning creatures?

2. The plants have not so much as the use of appearances, therefore we speak not of the Good in their regard. The Good, then, needs the power of using appearances. And this alone? Nay; for if so, say then that Good and Happiness and Unhappiness are with the lower animals too. But this you will not say, and you are right; for though they possessed the use of appearances in the highest degree, yet the observing and considering of this use they do not possess, and naturally so, for they exist to serve others, nor have any supreme object in themselves.[1] For the ass was not made for any supreme object in himself? Nay, but he was made able to bear, because we had need of a back; and, by Zeus, we had need moreover that he should walk; wherefore he received also the power to use appearances, else had he not been able to walk. And thereupon the matter stopped. For had he also received the observing and considering of the use of appearances, it is clear that in reason he could no longer have been subject to us, nor have served those needs of ours, but he had been our equal and our like.

3. For use is one thing, and observation and study is another. God had need of the other animals to use appearances, but of us to observe and study appearances. Wherefore it is enough for them to eat and drink, and rest and breed, and do whatever else each of them performs, but to us, to whom the faculty of observing and studying hath also been given, these things are not enough; but unless we act after a certain manner and ordinance, and conformably to the nature and constitution of man, we shall never attain the end of our being. For where the constitution is different, different there also is the task and the end. When, therefore, the constitution is one for use alone, then the use, of whatever kind it be, is enough; but where there is also observing and studying of the use, then, unless the due employment of this faculty be added, the end shall never be gained. What then? God hath constituted every other animal, one to be eaten, another to serve for tilling the land, another to yield cheese, another to some kindred use; for which things what need is there of the observing and studying of appearances, and the ability to make distinctions in them? But man he hath brought in to be a spectator of God and of His works, and not a spectator alone, but an interpreter of them. Wherefore it is shameful for a man to begin and to end where creatures do that are without Reason; but rather should he begin when they begin, and end where Nature ends in ourselves. But she ends in contemplation, in observing and studying, in a manner of life that is in harmony with Nature. See to it

then that ye die not without having been spectators of these things.

4. Seek, then, the essence of the Good there, where if it be not, thou wilt not say that the Good is in any other thing.

5. But what? are not those creatures also works of God? Surely; yet not supreme objects, yet not parts of the Gods. But thou art a supreme object, thou art a piece of God, thou hast in thee something that is a portion of Him. Why, then, art thou ignorant of thy high ancestry? Why knowest thou not whence thou camest? Wilt thou not remember, in thine eating, who it is that eats, and whom thou dost nourish? in cohabiting, who it is that cohabits? in converse, in exercise, in argument, knowest thou not that thou art nourishing a God, exercising a God? Unhappy man! thou bearest about with thee a God, and knowest it not! Thinkest thou I speak of some God of gold and silver, and external to thee? Nay, but in thyself thou dost bear him, and seest not that thou defilest him with thine impure thoughts and filthy deeds. In the presence even of an image of God thou hadst not dared to do one of those things which thou dost. But in the presence of God himself within thee, who seeth and heareth all things, thou art not ashamed of the things thou dost both desire and do, O thou unwitting of thine own nature, and subject to the wrath of God!

6. Why, then, do we fear in sending forth a young man from the school into some of the business of life, lest he should do wrong in anything, and be

luxurious or profligate, and lest a wrapping of rags degrade him, or fine raiment uplift him? Such a one knoweth not his own God, nor with whom he is setting out. But can we have patience with him, saying, *Would that I had you with me!*² And hast thou not God with thee there? or having Him, dost thou seek for any other? or will He speak other things to thee than even these?

7. But wert thou a statue of Pheidias, an Athena or Zeus, then wert thou mindful both of thyself and of the artist; and if thou hadst any consciousness, thou wouldst strive to do nothing unworthy of thy maker nor of thyself, nor ever to appear in any unseemly guise. But now that Zeus hath made thee, thou carest therefore nothing what kind of creature thou showest thyself for? And yet, is the one Artist like the other artist, or the one work like the other work? And what kind of work is that which hath in itself the faculties that were manifest in the making of it? Do not artists work in stone or brass or gold or ivory? and the Athena of Pheidias, when she hath once stretched out her hand and received upon it the figure of Victory, standeth thus for all time? But the works of God have motion and breathing, and the use of appearances and the judgment of them. Wilt thou dishonour such a Maker, whose work thou art? Nay, for not only did He make thee, but to thee alone did He trust and commit thyself. Wilt thou not remember this too, or wilt thou dishonour thy charge? But if God had committed some orphan child to thee, wouldst thou have neglected it?

## GOD IN MAN.

Now he hath given thee to thyself, and saith, *I had none more worthy of trust than thee; keep this man such as he was made by nature—reverent, faithful, high, unterrified, unshaken of passions, untroubled.* And thou wilt not.

8. But they may say : *Whence doth this fellow bring us that eye of scorn and solemn looks?* I have it not yet as I should. For I am yet unbold in those things which I have learned and assented to ; I yet fear my weakness. But let me be bold in them, and then ye shall see such a look, such a guise, as behoveth me to wear. Then shall I show you the statue when it is perfected and polished. What look ye for ?—an eye of scorn ? God forbid! For doth the Zeus in Olympia look scornfully ?—nay, but his glance is steadfast, as becometh him who will say,

"None trusts in vain my irrevocable word."—*Il.* i. 526.

Such will I show myself to you—faithful, reverent, generous, untroubled. *Not also, then, deathless, ageless, diseaseless?* Nay, but dying as God, sickening as a God. These I have, these I can ; but other things I neither have nor can. I will show you the thews of a philosopher. And what are these ? A pursuit that never fails, an avoidance that never miscarries, seemly desire, studious resolve, cautious assent.[8] These shall ye see.

## CHAPTER V.

OF DIVINATION.[1]

1. WHEN thou goest to inquire of an oracle, remember that what the event will be thou knowest not, for this is the thing thou art come to learn from the seer; but of what nature it is (if haply thou art a philosopher), thou knewest already in coming. For if it be any of those things that are not in our own power, it follows of necessity that it can be neither good nor evil.

2. Bring, therefore, to the seer neither pursuit nor avoidance, nor go before him with trembling, but well knowing that all events are indifferent and nothing to thee. For whatever it may be, it shall lie with thee to use it nobly; and this no man can prevent. Go, then, with a good courage to the Gods as to counsellors; and for the rest, when anything hath been counselled thee, remember of whom thou hast taken counsel, and whom thou wilt be slighting if thou art not obedient.

3. Therefore, as Socrates would have it, go to the oracle for those matters only where thy whole inquiry bendeth solely towards the event, and where there are no means either from reason or any other art for knowing beforehand what is to happen. Thus, when it may be needful to share some peril with thy friend or thy country, inquire of no oracle whether thou shouldst do the thing. For if the seer should

declare that the sacrifices are inauspicious, this signifies clearly either death, or the loss of some limb, or banishment; yet doth Reason decree that even so thou must stand by thy friend, and share thy country's danger.

4. Mark, therefore, that greater seer, the Pythian, who cast out of his temple one that, when his friend was being murdered, did not help him.[2]

END OF BOOK IV.

# BOOK V.

## CHAPTER I.

### THE BEHAVIOUR OF A PHILOSOPHER.

1. ORDAIN for thyself forthwith a certain form and type of conduct, which thou shalt maintain both alone and, when it may chance, among men.

2. And for the most part keep silence, or speak only what is necessary, and in few words. But when occasion may call thee to speak, then speak, but sparingly, and not about any subject at hap-hazard, nor about gladiators, nor horse races, nor athletes, nor things to eat and drink, which are talked of everywhere; but, above all, not about men, as blaming or praising or comparing them.

If, then, thou art able, let thy discourse draw that of the company towards what is seemly and good. But if thou find thyself apart among men of another sort, keep silence.

3. Laugh not much, nor at many things, nor unrestrainedly.

4. Refuse altogether, if thou canst, to take an oath; if thou canst not, then as the circumstances allow.[1]

5. Shun banquets given by strangers and by the

vulgar. But if any occasion bring thee to them, give strictest heed, lest thou fall unawares into the ways of the vulgar. For know that if thy companion be corrupt, he who hath conversation with him must needs be corrupted also, even if himself should chance to be pure.

6. Hath any of you the art of a lute-player when he takes the lute in his hand, so as at once when he hath touched the strings to know which are out of tune, and then to tune the instrument?—such a gift as Socrates had, who in every company could lead those that were with him to his own topic? Whence should you have it? but ye must needs be carried about hither and thither by the vulgar. And wherefore, then, are they stronger than ye? For that they speak their sorry stuff from belief; but ye, your fine talk from the lips out. Wherefore it is flat and dead; and sickening it is to hear your exhortations and this wretched virtue of yours, which is prated of in every quarter. And thus the vulgar conquer you. For everywhere belief is mighty, belief is invincible. Until then the right opinions are hardened in you; and until ye shall have gained a certain strength for your safety, I counsel you to mingle cautiously with the vulgar, else every day, like wax in the sun, shall whatever hath been written in you in the school be melted away.

7. In things that concern the body accept only so far as the bare need—as in food, drink, clothing, habitation, servants. But all that makes for glory or luxury thou must utterly proscribe.

8. Concerning intercourse of the sexes, it is right to be pure before marriage, to the best of thy power. But, using it, let a man have to do only with what is lawful. Yet be not grievous to those who use such pleasures, nor censorious; nor be often putting thyself forward as not using them.

9. If one shall bear thee word that such a one hath spoken evil of thee, then do not defend thyself against his accusations, but make answer: *He little knew my other vices, or he had not mentioned only these.*

10. There is no necessity to go often to the arena, but if occasion should take thee there, do not appear ardent on any man's side but thine own; that is to say, choose that only to happen which does happen, and that the conqueror may be simply he who wins; for so shalt thou not be thwarted. But from shouting and laughing at this or that, or violent gesticulation, thou must utterly abstain. And when thou art gone away, converse little on the things that have passed, so far as they make not for thine own correction. For from that it would appear that admiration of the spectacle had overcome thee.

11. Go not freely nor indiscriminately to recitations.[2] But if thou go, then preserve (yet without being grievous to others) thy gravity and calmness.

12. When thou art about to meet anyone, especially one of those that are thought high in rank, set before thy mind what Socrates or Zéno had done in such a case. And so thou wilt not fail to deal as it behoves thee with the occasion.

13. When thou goest to any of those that are great

in power, set before thy mind the case that thou wilt not find him at home, that thou wilt be shut out, that the doors may be slammed in thy face, that he will take no notice of thee. And if even with these things it behoves thee to go, then go, and bear all that happens; and never say to thyself—*It was not worth this.* For that is the part of the foolish, and of those that are offended at outward things.

14. In company, be it far from thee to dwell much and over-measure on thine own deeds and dangers. For to dwell on thine own dangers is pleasant indeed to thee, but not equally pleasant for others is it to hear of the things that have chanced to thee.

15. Be it far from thee to move laughter. For that habit is a slippery descent into vulgarity;[3] and it is always enough to relax thy neighbours' respect for thee.

16. And it is dangerous to approach to vicious conversation. Therefore, when anything of the kind may arise, rebuke, if there is opportunity, him who approacheth thereto. But if not, then at least by silence and blushing and grave looks, let it be plain that his talk is disagreeable to thee,

## CHAPTER II.

### ON HABIT.

1. EVERY skill and faculty is maintained and increased by the corresponding acts; as, the faculty of

walking by walking, of running by running. If you will read aloud well, then do it constantly; if you will write, then write. But when you have not read aloud for thirty days together, but done something else, you shall see the result. Thus, if you have lain down for ten days, then rise up and endeavour to walk a good distance, and you shall see how your legs are enfeebled. In general, then, if you would make yourself skilled in anything, then do it; and if you would refrain from anything, then do it not, but use yourself to do rather some other thing instead of it.

2. And thus it is in spiritual things also. When thou art wrathful, know that not this single evil hath happened to thee, but that thou hast increased the aptness to it, and, as it were, poured oil upon the fire. When thou art overcome in passion, think not that this defeat is all; but thou hast nourished thine incontinence, and increased it. For it is impossible but that aptitudes and faculties should spring up where they were not before, or spread and grow mightier, by the corresponding acts. And thus, surely, do also, as the philosophers say, the infirmities of the soul grow up. For when thou hast once been covetous of money, if Reason, which leadeth to a sense of the vice, be called to aid, then both the desire is set at rest, and our ruling faculty is re-established, as it was in the beginning. But if thou bring no remedy to aid, then shall the soul return no more to the first estate; but when next excited by the corresponding appearance, shall be kindled to desire even more

## ON HABIT.

quickly than before. And when this is continually happening, the soul becomes callous in the end, and through its infirmity the love of money is strengthened. For he that hath had a fever, when the illness hath left him, is not what he was before his fever, unless he have been entirely healed. And somewhat on this wise also it happens in the affections of the soul; certain traces and scars are left in it, the which if a man do not wholly eradicate, when he hath been again scourged on the same place, it shall make no longer scars, but sores.

3. Wouldst thou, then, be no longer of a wrathful temper? Then do not nourish the aptness to it, give it nothing that will increase it, be tranquil from the outset, and number the days when thou hast not been wrathful. *I have not been wrathful now for one, now for two, now for three days;* but if thou have saved thirty days, then sacrifice to God. For the aptness is at first enfeebled, and then destroyed. *To-day I was not vexed, nor to-morrow, nor for two or three months together; but I was heedful when anything happened to move me thus.* Know that thou art in good case. To-day, when I saw a fair woman, I did not say to myself, *Would that one could possess her;* nor, *Happy is her husband,* for he who saith this saith also, *Happy is her paramour;* nor do I picture to my mind what should follow. But I stroke my head, and say, *Well done, Epictetus! you have solved a fine sophism, finer by far than the master sophism.* But if she were also willing and consenting, and sent to me, and if she also laid hold of me, and drew near to me, and I should yet

restrain myself and conquer, this were indeed then a sophism above the Liar, above the Quiescent. Verily, for this a man's spirit may rightly swell, and not for propounding the master sophism.[1]

4. How, then, may this come to pass? Resolve at last to seek thine own commendation, to appear fair in the eyes of God; desire to become pure with thine own pure self, and with God. Then when thou shalt fall in with any appearance such as we have spoken of, what saith Plato? *Go to the purifying sacrifices, go and pray in the temples of the protecting Gods.*[2] It shall even suffice if thou seek the company of good and wise men, and try thyself by one of them, whether he be one of the living or of the dead.

5. By opposing these remedies thou shalt conquer the appearance, nor be led captive by it. But at the outset, be not swept away by the vehemence of it; but say, *Await me a little, thou appearance; let me see what thou art, and with what thou hast to do; let me approve thee.* And then permit it not to lead thee forward, and to picture to thee what should follow, else it shall take possession of thee, and carry thee whithersoever it will. But rather bring in against it some other fair and noble appearance, and therewithal cast out this vile one. And if thou use to exercise thyself in this way, thou shalt see what shoulders and nerves and sinews thou wilt have! But now we have only wordiness, and nothing more.

6. This is the true athlete,[3] he who exerciseth himself against such appearances. Hold, unhappy man! be not swept away. Great is the contest, divine the

task, for kingship, for freedom, for prosperity, for tranquillity. Be mindful of God, call Him to be thy helper and defender, as men at sea call upon the Dioscuri in a storm.⁴ For what greater tempest is there than that which proceedeth from appearances, that mightily overcome and expel the Reason? Yea, a storm itself, what is it but an appearance? For, take away only the dread of death, and bring as many thunderings and lightnings as thou wilt, and thou shalt see what fair weather and calm there will be in the ruling faculty. But if having been once defeated, thou shalt say, *The next time I will conquer;* and then the same thing over again, be sure that in the end thou wilt be brought to such a sorry and feeble state that henceforth thou wilt not so much as know that thou art sinning; but thou wilt begin to make excuses for the thing, and then confirm that saying of Hesiod to be true:—

"With ills unending strives the putter off."
—*Works and Days*, 411.

7. What then? can a man make this resolve, and so stand up faultless? He cannot; but this much he can—to be ever straining towards faultlessness. For happy it were if, by never relaxing this industrious heed, we shall rid ourselves of at least a few of our faults. But now, when thou sayest, *From to-morrow I shall be heedful,* know that this is what thou art saying:—*To-day I shall be shameless, importunate, abject; it shall be in others' power to afflict me; to-day I shall be wrathful, envious.* Lo, to how many vices

dost thou give place! But if aught be well to-morrow, how much better to-day? if to-morrow suit, how much better to-day? Yea, and for this, too, that thou mayest have the power to-morrow, and not again put it off till the third day.

## CHAPTER III.

### ON DISPUTATION.

1. WHAT things a man must have learned in order to be able to reason well have been accurately defined by our philosophers; but in the fitting use of them we are wholly unexercised. Give any one of us whom ye please some ignorant man for a disputant, and he shall find no way to deal with him; but if, when he hath moved him a little, the man answer beside the purpose, he is no longer able to manage him, but either he will revile him, or mock him, and say, *He is an ignorant fellow; nothing can be done with him.*

2. But a guide, when he hath found one straying from the way, leads him into the proper road, and does not mock him or revile him, and then go away. And do thou show such a man the truth, and thou shalt see that he will follow it. But so long as thou dost not show it, mock him not, but be sensible rather of thine own incapacity.

3. But what? this business of instruction is not very

safe at present, and least of all in Rome; for he who pursues it will of course feel constrained not to do it in a corner, but he must go to some man of consular rank, it may be, or some rich man, and inquire of him: Sir, can you tell me to whom you have committed the care of your horses? *Surely.* Was it, then, to any chance-comer and one inexperienced about horses? *By no means.* Well then, to whom are your gold and silver vessels and raiment entrusted? *Neither are these committed to any chance person.* And your body, have you already sought out one to whom to commit the care of it? *How not?* And that also one who is experienced in training and medicine? *Assuredly.* Whether, now, are these the best things you have, or do you possess aught that is better than all of them? *What thing do you mean?* That, by Zeus, which useth all these, and approveth each of them and taketh counsel? *Is it the soul, then, that you mean?* You have conceived me rightly; it is even this. *Truly I hold that I possess in this something much better than everything else.* Can you then declare to us in what manner you have taken thought for your soul? for it is not likely that a wise man like yourself, and one of repute in the State, would overlook the best thing you possess, and use no diligence or design about it, but leave it neglected and perishing? *Surely not.* But do you provide for it yourself? and have you learned the way from another, or discovered it yourself?

4. And then at last there is danger lest he say first, *Good sir, what is this to you? who are you?* and then, if you persist in troubling him, that he may lift up his

hands and smite you. Once I too was an admirer of this method until I fell into these difficulties.

## CHAPTER IV.

### THAT WE SHOULD BE SLOW IN ACCEPTING PLEASURE.

1. WHEN thou hast received the appearance of some pleasure, then, as in other things, guard thyself lest thou be carried away by it, but delay with thyself a little, and let the thing await thee for a while. Then bethink thyself of the two periods of time, one when thou shalt be enjoying the pleasure, the other, when, having enjoyed it, thou shalt afterwards repent of it and reproach thyself. And set on the other side how thou shalt rejoice and commend thyself if thou abstain.

2. But if it seem reasonable to thee to do the thing, beware lest thou have been conquered by the flattery and the sweetness and the allurement of it. But set on the other side how much better were the consciousness of having won that victory.

## CHAPTER V.

### THAT WE SHOULD BE OPEN IN OUR DEALINGS.

IN doing aught which thou hast clearly discerned as right to do, seek never to avoid being seen in the doing of it, even though the multitude should be destined to form some wrong opinion concerning it. For if thou dost not right, avoid the deed itself. But if rightly, why fear those who will wrongly rebuke thee?

## CHAPTER VI.

### THAT HALF TRUE MAY BE ALL FALSE.

As the sayings, *It is day*, *It is night*, are wholly justifiable if viewed disjunctively,[1] but not if viewed together, even so at a feast, to pick out the largest portion for oneself may be justifiable, if we look to the needs of the body alone, but is unjustifiable if viewed as it concerns the preservation of the proper community in the feast. Therefore, in eating with another person, remember not to look only at the value for the body of the things that are set before thee, but to preserve also the reverence due to the giver of the feast.

## CHAPTER VII.

### THAT EACH MAN PLAY HIS OWN PART.

1. If thou hast assumed a part beyond thy power to play, then thou hast both come to shame in that, and missed one thou couldst have well performed.

2. And some one having inquired, *How, then, shall each of us perceive what character he befits?* Whence, said Epictetus, doth the bull alone, when the lion approacheth, discover his own capacity, and advance to defend the whole herd? It is clear that with the capacity is ever joined the perception of the same, and thus, whoever of us may possess a like capacity will not be ignorant of it. But a bull is not made in a moment, nor is a man of generous spirit; but we must have preparation and winter-training,[1] and not lightly rush upon things that do not concern us.

---

## CHAPTER VIII.

### THAT WE SHOULD BE CAREFUL OF THE SOUL AS OF THE BODY.

In going about, you are careful not to step upon a nail or to twist your foot. Care thus also, lest you injure your ruling faculty. And if we observe this in each thing we do, we shall the more safely undertake it.

---

## CHAPTER IX.

### THE MEASURE OF GAIN.

The measure of gain for each man is the body, as the foot is for the shoe. Take your stand on this, and you shall preserve the measure. But if you transgress it, you must thenceforth be borne, as it were, down a steep. And so it is with the shoe, for if you will go beyond the measure of the foot, the shoe will be first gilded, then dyed purple, then embroidered. For that which hath once transgressed its measure hath no longer any limit.

## CHAPTER X.

### THE WORTH OF WOMEN.

FROM the age of fourteen years women are flattered and worshipped by men. Seeing thus that there is nothing else for them but to serve the pleasure of men, they begin to beautify themselves, and to place all their hopes in this. It were well, then, that they should perceive themselves to be prized for nothing else than modesty and decorum.

## CHAPTER XI.

### A DULL NATURE.

IT betokens a dull nature to be greatly occupied in matters that concern the body, as to be much concerned about exercising oneself, or eating, or drinking, or other bodily acts. But these things should be done by the way, and all attention be given to the mind.

## CHAPTER XII.

### OF ADORNMENT OF THE PERSON.

1. A CERTAIN young man, a rhetorician, having come to Epictetus with his hair dressed in an unusually elaborate way, and his other attire much adorned, Tell me, said Epictetus, think you not that some dogs are beautiful, and some horses, and so of the other animals?

——" I do think it," said he.

And men too—are not some beautiful and some ill-favoured?

——" How otherwise ?"

Whether, then, do we call each of these beautiful for the same reasons and in the same kind, or each for something proper to itself? And you shall see the matter thus: Inasmuch as we observe a dog to be formed by nature for one end, and a horse for another, and, let us say, a nightingale for another, we may in general say, not unreasonably, that each of them is then beautiful when it is excellent according to its own nature; but since the nature of each is different,

different also, it seems to me, is the manner of being beautiful in each. Is it not so?
He acknowledged that it was.
Therefore, that which maketh a dog beautiful maketh a horse ill-favoured; and that which maketh a horse beautiful, a dog ill-favoured; if, indeed, their natures are different?
—— " So it seems."
And that which maketh a beautiful Pancratiast,[1] the same maketh a wrestler not good, and a runner utterly laughable. And he who is beautiful for the Pentathlon is very bad for wrestling?
—— " It is so," he said.
What is it, then, that makes a man beautiful? Is it not that which, in its kind, makes also a dog or a horse beautiful?
—— " It is that," he answered.
What, then, makes a dog beautiful? The presence of the virtue of a dog. And a horse? The presence of the virtue of a horse. And what, then, a man? Is it not also the presence of the virtue of a man? And, O youth, if thou wouldst be beautiful, do thou labour to perfect this, the virtue of a human being. But what is it? Look whom you praise when you praise any without affection—is it the righteous or the unrighteous?
—— " The righteous."
Is it the temperate or the profligate?
—— " The temperate."
Is it the continent or the incontinent?
—— " The continent."

Then making yourself such a one as you praise, you will know that you are making yourself beautiful; but so long as you neglect these things, though you sought out every device to appear beautiful, you must of necessity be ugly.

2. For thou art not flesh and hair, but a Will: if thou keep this beautiful, then wilt thou be beautiful. But so far I dare not tell thee that thou art ugly, for I think thou wilt more easily bear to hear anything else than this. But see what Socrates saith to Alcibiades, the most beautiful and blooming of men: *Endeavour, then, to be beautiful;* and what saith he? *Curl thy locks, and pluck out the hairs of thy legs?* God forbid. But *set thy Will in order, cast out evil doctrines.*

——"And how then shall we deal with the body?"

As Nature made it. Another hath cared for this; commit it to Him.

——"But what? Shall the body then be uncleansed?"

God forbid. But that which thou art and wast made by Nature, cleanse this; let a man be clean as a man, a woman as a woman, a child as a child.

3. For we ought not even by the aspect of the body to scare away the multitude from philosophy; but by his body, as in all other things, a philosopher should show himself cheerful, and free from troubles. *Behold, friends, how I have nothing and need nothing; behold how I am homeless and landless, and an exile, if so it chance, and hearthless, and yet I live more free*

## ADORNMENT OF THE PERSON. 173

*from troubles than all the lordly and the rich. But look on my body, too; ye see that it is not the worse for my hard life.* But if one saith this to me, having the countenance and garb of a condemned criminal, what God shall persuade me to approach to philosophy which makes such men as this? God forbid! I would not, were it even to become a sage.

4. I, indeed, by the Gods, had rather a young man in his first movement towards philosophy came to me with his hair curled than dishevelled and foul. For a certain impression of the beautiful is to be seen in him; and an aim at what is becoming, and to the thing wherein it seemeth to him to lie, there he applies his art. Thenceforth it only needs to show him its true place, and to say, *Young man, thou seekest the beautiful, and thou dost well. Know, then, that it flourishes there where thy Reason is; there seek it where are thy likes and dislikes, thy pursuits and avoidances, for this is what thou hast in thyself of choice and precious, but the body is by nature mud. Why dost thou spend thy labour upon it in vain? for that the body is naught, Time shall certainly teach thee, though it teach thee nothing else.* But if one come to me foul and filthy, and a moustache down to the knees, what have I to say to him? with what image or likeness can I draw him on? For with what that is like unto Beauty hath he ever busied himself, so as I may set him on another course, and say, *Not here is Beauty, but there?* Will you have me tell him, *Beauty consists not in being befouled, but in the Reason?* For doth he even seek Beauty? hath he any

impression of it in his mind? Go, and reason with a hog, that he shall not roll himself in the mud.

5. Behold a youth worthy of love—behold an old man worthy to love, and to be loved in return; to whom one may commit his sons, his daughters, to be taught; to whom young men may come, if it please you—that he may deliver lectures to them on a dunghill! God forbid. Every extravagance arises from something in human nature, but this is near to being one that is not human.

## CHAPTER XIII.

### WHY WE SHOULD BEAR WITH WRONG.

WHEN some one may do you an injury, or speak ill of you, remember that he either does it or speaks it believing that it is right and meet for him to do so. It is not possible, then, that he can follow the thing that appears to you, but the thing that appears to him. Wherefore, if it appear evil to him, it is he that is injured, being deceived. For also if any one should take a true consequence to be false, it is not the consequence that is injured, but he which is deceived. Setting out, then, from these opinions, you will bear a gentle mind towards any man who may revile you. For, say on each occasion, *So it appeared to him.*

## CHAPTER XIV.

#### THAT EVERYTHING HATH TWO HANDLES.

EVERY matter hath two handles—by the one it may be carried; by the other, not. If thy brother do thee wrong, take not this thing by the handle, *He wrongs me;* for that is the handle whereby it may not be carried. But take it rather by the handle, *He is my brother, nourished with me;* and thou wilt take it by a handle whereby it may be carried.


## CHAPTER XV.

#### ON CERTAIN FALSE CONCLUSIONS.

THERE is no true conclusion in these reasonings : *I am richer than thou, therefore I am better: I am more eloquent than thou, therefore I am better.* But the conclusions are rather these: *I am richer than thou, therefore my wealth is better: I am more eloquent than thou, therefore my speech is better.* But thou art not wealth, and thou art not speech.

## CHAPTER XVI.

#### PERCEPTION AND JUDGMENT.

1. Doth a man bathe himself quickly? Then, say not, *Wrongly,* but *Quickly.* Doth he drink much wine? Then say not, *Wrongly,* but *Much.* For whence do you know if it were ill done till you have understood his opinion?

2. Thus it shall not befall you to assent to any other things than those whereof you are truly and directly sensible.[1]

3. What is the cause of assenting to anything? The appearance that it is so. But if it appear to be not so, it is impossible to assent to it. Wherefore? For that this is the nature of the mind, to receive the true with favour, the false with disfavour, and the uncertain with indifference. The proof of this? Be sure, if you can, at this moment, that it is night. You cannot. Cease to be sure that it is day. You cannot. Be sure that the stars are odd in number, or that they are even. You cannot. When, therefore, any man shall assent to what is false, know that he had no will to consent to falsehood; for, as saith Plato, no soul is willingly deprived of the truth, but the false appeared to it to be true. Come, then, what have we in actions corresponding to this true and false? The seemly and the unseemly, the profitable and the unprofitable, that which concerns me and that which doth not concern me, and such like. Can

any man think that a certain thing is for his profit, and not elect to do it? He cannot. How, then, is it with her who saith—

> "And well I know the evils I shall do,
> But wrath is lord of all my purposes?"—*Medea*, 1079.

For, did she hold this very thing, to gratify her wrath and avenge herself on her husband, more profitable than to spare her children? Even so: but she was deceived. Show her clearly that she was deceived, and she will not do it; but so long as you show it not, what else hath she to follow than the thing as it appears to her? Nothing. Wherefore, then, have you indignation with her, that the unhappy wretch has gone astray concerning the greatest things, and has become a viper instead of a human being? If anything, will you not rather pity, as we pity the blind and the lame, those that are blinded and lamed in the chiefest of their faculties?

4. ——"So that all these great and dreadful deeds have this same origin in the appearance of the thing?"

The same, and no other. The *Iliad* is nought but appearance, and the use of appearances. The thing that appeared to Paris was the carrying off of the wife of Menelaus; the thing that appeared to Helen was to accompany him. Had it, then, appeared to Menelaus to be sensible that it was a gain to be deprived of such a wife, what would have happened? Not only had there been no *Iliad*, but no *Odyssey* neither.

—— "On such a little thing do such great ones hang?"

But what talk is this of great things? Wars and seditions and destructions of many men, and overthrow of cities? And what is there of great in these? Nothing. For what is there of greatness in the deaths of many oxen and sheep, and the burning or overthrow of many nests of swallows or storks?

—— "But are these things like unto those?"

They are most like. The bodies of men are destroyed, and the bodies of oxen and of sheep. The dwellings of men are burned, and the nests of storks. What is there great, what is there awful in this? Or show me wherein differeth the dwelling of a man, as a dwelling, from the nest of a stork, save that the one buildeth his little houses of planks and tiles and bricks, and the other of sticks and mud?

—— "Are a stork and a man, then, alike?"

What say you? In body they are most like.

—— "Doth a man, then, differ in no respect from a stork?"

God forbid; but in these matters there is no difference.

—— "Wherein, then, doth he differ?"

Seek, and you shall find that in another thing there is a difference. Look if it be not in the observing and studying of what he doth; look if it be not in his social instinct, in his faith, his reverence, his steadfastness, his understanding. Where, then, is the great Good or Evil for man? There, where the difference is. If this be saved, and abide, as it were, in a fortress, and reverence be not depraved, nor faith nor understanding, then is the man also saved. But if one of these things perish, or be taken by storm, then doth the man also perish. And in this it is that great actions are done. It was a mighty downfall, they say, for Paris, when the Greeks came, and when they sacked Troy, and when his brothers perished. Not so: for through another's act can no man fall—that was the sacking of the storks' nests. But the downfall was then when he lost reverence and faith, when he betrayed hospitality and violated decorum. When was the fall of Achilles? When Patroclus died? God forbid; but when he was wrathful, when he bewept the loss of his girl, when he forgot that he was there not to win mistresses but to make war. These, for men, are downfall and storming and overthrow, when right opinions are demolished or depraved.

## CHAPTER XVII.

### THAT THE PHILOSOPHER SHALL EXHIBIT TO THE VULGAR DEEDS, NOT WORDS.

1. THOU shalt never proclaim thyself a philosopher, nor speak much among the vulgar of the philosophic maxims; but do the things that follow from the maxims. For example, do not discourse at a feast upon how one ought to eat, but eat as one ought.

For remember that even so Socrates everywhere banished ostentation, so that men used to come to him desiring that he would recommend them to teachers of philosophy, and he brought them away and did so, so well did he bear to be overlooked.

2. And if among the vulgar discourse should arise concerning some maxim of thy philosophy, do thou, for the most part, keep silence, for there is great risk that thou straightway vomit up what thou hast not digested. And when someone shall say to thee, *Thou knowest naught*, and it bites thee not, then know that thou hast begun the work.

3. And as sheep do not bring their food to the shepherds to show how much they have eaten, but digesting inwardly their provender, bear outwardly wool and milk, even so do not thou, for the most part, display the maxims before the vulgar, but rather the works which follow from them when they are digested.

## CHAPTER XVIII.

### ASCESIS.

WHEN you have adapted the body to a frugal way of living, do not flatter yourself on that, nor if you drink only water, say, on every opportunity, *I drink only water*. And if you desire at any time to inure yourself to labour and endurance, do it to yourself and not unto the world. And do not embrace the statues; but some time when you are exceedingly thirsty take a mouthful of cold water, and spit it out, and say nothing about it.

## CHAPTER XIX.

### TOKENS.

1. THE position and token of the vulgar: he looks never to himself for benefit or hurt, but always to outward things. The position and character of the philosopher: he looks for benefit or hurt only to himself.

2. The tokens of one that is making advance: he blames none, he praises none, he accuses none, he complains of none; he speaks never of himself, as being somewhat, or as knowing aught. When he is thwarted or hindered in aught, he accuseth himself. If one should praise him, he laughs at him in his sleeve; if one should blame him, he makes no defence. He goes about like the sick and feeble, fearing to move the parts that are settling together before they have taken hold. He hath taken out of himself all pursuit, and hath turned all avoidance to things in our power which are contrary to nature. Toward all things he will keep his inclination slack. If he is thought foolish or unlearned, he regardeth it not. In a word, he watches himself as he would a treacherous enemy.

## CHAPTER XX.

#### THAT THE LOGICAL ART IS NECESSARY.

1. SINCE Reason is that by which all other things are organised and perfected,[1] it is meet that itself should not remain unorganised. But by what shall it be organised? For it is clear that this must be either by itself or by some other thing. But this must be Reason; or something else which is greater than Reason, which is impossible.

2. "Yea," one may say, "but it is more pressing to cure our vices, and the like."

You desire, then, to hear something of these things? Hear then; but if you shall say to me, *I know not if you are reasoning truly or falsely?* or if I utter something ambiguous, and you shall bid me distinguish, shall I lose patience with you and tell you, *It is more pressing to cure our vices than chop logic?*

3. For this reason I think the logical arts are set at the beginning of our study, even as before the measuring of corn we set the examination of the measure. For unless we shall first establish what is a modius[2] and what is a balance, how shall we be able to measure or weigh anything?

4. In this case, then, if you have not understood and accurately investigated the criterion of all other things, and that through which they are understood, shall we be able to investigate and understand anything else? and how could we? *Yea, but a modius*

is a wooden thing, and barren. But it measures corn. And logic is also barren. As regards this, indeed, we shall see. But even if one should grant this, it sufficeth that logic is that which distinguishes and investigates other things, and, as one may say, measures and weighs them. Who saith these things? is it Chrysippus alone and Zeno and Cleanthes? but doth not Antisthenes[3] say it? And who wrote that the investigation of terms is the beginning of education? —was it not Socrates? and of whom doth Xenophon write that he began with the investigation of terms, what each of them signified?

## CHAPTER XXI.

### GRAMMARIAN OR SAGE.

WHEN some one may exalt himself in that he is able to understand and expound the works of Chrysippus, say then to thyself: If Chrysippus had not written obscurely, this man would have had nothing whereon to exalt himself. But I, what do I desire? Is it not to learn to understand Nature and to follow her? I inquire, then, who can expound Nature to me, and hearing that Chrysippus can, I betake myself to him. But I do not understand his writings, therefore I seek an expounder for them. And so far there is nothing exalted. But when I have found the expounder, it remaineth for me to put in practice what he declares to me, and in this alone is there anything exalted. But if I shall admire the bare exposition, what else have I made of myself than a grammarian instead of a philosopher, save, indeed, that the exposition is of Chrysippus and not of Homer? When, therefore, one may ask me to lecture on the philosophy of Chrysippus, I shall rather blush when I am not able to show forth works of a like nature and in harmony with the words.

## CHAPTER XXII.

### ACCOMPLISHMENTS.

1. THE clearer be the characters in which a book is writ, the more pleasantly and conveniently shall any man read it. Thus also a man shall listen more conveniently to any discourse if it be conveyed in well-ordered and graceful words. Be it not said, then, that there is no faculty of expression, for this is the thought of a man both impious and cowardly[1] —impious, for he holds in disesteem the gracious gifts of God, as if he would take away the serviceable faculty of seeing, or of hearing, or indeed this of speaking. Did God give thee eyes for nothing? And was it for nothing that He mingled in them a spirit of such might and cunning as to reach a long

# ACCOMPLISHMENTS.

way off and receive the impression of visible forms—a messenger so swift and faithful? Was it for nothing that He gave the intervening air such efficacy, and made it elastic, so that being, in a manner, strained,[2] our vision should traverse it? Was it for nothing that He made Light, without which there were no benefit of any other thing?

2. Man, be not unthankful for these things, nor yet unmindful of better things. For seeing and hearing, and, by Zeus, for life itself, and the things that work together to maintain it, for dried fruits, for wine, for oil, do thou give thanks to God. But remember that He hath given thee another thing which is better than all these—that, namely, which uses them, which approves them, which taketh account of the worth of each. For what is that which declareth concerning all these faculties how much each of them is worth? Is it the faculty itself? Heard you ever the faculty of vision tell aught concerning itself? or that of hearing? or wheat, or barley, or a horse, or a dog? Nay, but as ministers and slaves are they appointed, to serve the faculty which makes use of appearances. And if you would learn how much any of them is worth, of whom will you inquire? who shall give answer? How then shall any other faculty be greater than this, which both useth the others as its servants, and the same approveth each of them and declareth concerning them? For which of them knoweth what itself is, and what it is worth? Which of them knoweth when it behoves to make use of it, and when not? What is that which openeth and closeth the eyes, turning them

away from things which they should not behold, and guiding them towards other things? Is it the faculty of vision? Nay, but the faculty of the Will. What is that which closeth and openeth the ears?—that in obedience to which they become busy and curious, or, again, unmoved by what they hear? Is it the faculty of hearing? It is no other than that of the Will.

3. Being then so great a faculty, and set over all the rest, let it come to us and tell us that the best of existing things is the flesh! Not even if the flesh itself affirmed that it was the best, would any man have patience with it. Now what is it, Epicurus, which declares this doctrine, that the flesh is best, which wrote concerning the *End of Being*, and on *Laws of Nature*, and on the *Canon of Truth?*—which let thy beard grow? which wrote, when dying, that it was spending its last day and a happy one?[3] Is it the flesh or the Will? Wilt thou affirm, then, that thou hast aught better than the Will? Nay, but art thou not mad—so blind, in truth, and deaf as thou art?

4. What then? Shall any man contemn the other faculties? God forbid! Doth any man say that there is no use or eminence in the faculty of eloquence. God forbid—that were senseless, impious, thankless towards God. But to each thing its true worth. For there is a certain use in an ass, but not so much as in an ox; and in a dog, but not so much as in a slave; and in a slave, but not so much as in a citizen; and in citizens, but not so much as in governors. Yet not because other things are better is the use which anything

affords to be contemned. There is a certain worth in the faculty of eloquence, but not so much as in the Will. When, then, I speak thus, let no man deem that I would have you neglect the power of eloquence, for I would not have you neglect your eyes, or ears, or hands, or feet, or raiment, or shoes. But if one ask me which is, then, the best of existing things, what shall I say? The faculty of eloquence I cannot say, but that of the Will, when it is made right. For this is that which useth the other, and all the other faculties, both small and great. When this is set right, a man that was not good becomes good; when it is not right, the man becomes evil. This is that whereby we fail or prosper—whereby we blame others, or approve them; the neglect of which is the misery, and the care of it the happiness, of mankind.

5. But to take away the faculty of eloquence, and to say that there is in truth no such faculty, is not only the part of a thankless man toward Him who hath given it, but also of a cowardly. For such a one seemeth to me to fear lest if there be any faculty of this kind we shall not be able to despise it. Such are they also which say that there is no difference between beauty and ugliness. Then were a man to be affected in like manner on seeing Thersites and Achilles, or on seeing Helen and any common woman? Truly, a thought of fools and boors, and of men who know not the nature of each thing, but fear lest, if one perceive the difference, he shall be straightway swept away and overpowered by it. But the great thing is this—to leave to each the faculty that it

hath, and so leaving it to scan the worth of the faculty, and to learn what is the greatest of existing things; and everywhere to pursue this, and be zealous about this, making all other things accessory to this, albeit, according to our powers, not neglecting even these.  For of the eyes also must we take care, yet not as of the best thing; yet of these, too, by the very exercise of the best thing; since that shall in no other wise subsist according to Nature save by wise dealing in these matters, and preferring certain things to others.

6. But what is done in the world? As if a man journeying to his own country should pass by an excellent inn, and the inn being agreeable to him, should stay, and abide in it. Man, thou hast forgotten thy purpose; thy journeying was not to this, but through this. *But this is pleasant.* And how many other inns are pleasant, and how many meadows? yet merely for passing through. But thy business is this, to arrive in thy native country, to remove the fears of thy kinsfolk, to do, thyself, the duties of a citizen, to marry, to beget children, to fill the customary offices. For thou art not come into this world to choose out its pleasanter places, but to dwell in those where thou wast born, and whereof thou wast appointed to be a citizen. And so in some wise it is with this matter. Since, by the aid of speech and such like deliverance, we must come to our aim, and purify the Will, and order aright the faculty which makes use of appearances; and it is necessary that this deliverance of the doctrines come to pass by a certain use of speech, and

with a certain art and trenchancy of expression, there are some which are taken captive by these things themselves, and abide in them—one in the gift of speech, one in syllogisms, one in sophisms, one in some such another of these inns, and there they linger and moulder away, as though they were fallen among the Sirens.

7. Man, thy business was to make thyself fit to use the appearances that encounter thee according to Nature, not missing what thou pursuest, nor falling into what thou wouldst avoid, never failing of good fortune, nor overtaken of ill fortune, free, unhindered, uncompelled, agreeing with the governance of Zeus, obedient unto the same, and well-pleased therein; blaming none, charging none, able of thy whole soul to utter those lines :—

"Lead me, O Zeus, and thou, Destiny!"

Then, having this for thy business, if some little matter of eloquence please thee, or certain speculations, wilt thou stay and abide in them, and elect to settle in them, forgetting all that is at home? and wilt thou say, *These things are admirable?* Who saith they are not admirable? but for passing through, like inns. What should hinder one that spoke like Demosthenes to be unfortunate? or one that could resolve syllogisms like Chrysippus to be miserable, to grieve, to envy; in a word, to be troubled and unhappy? Nothing. Thou seest now that all these things are but inns, and of no worth; but our business was another thing. When I say these things to certain persons, they think I am rejecting all care about language or speculation. But I do not reject this; I reject the endless occupation with them, the putting our hopes in them. If a man by this teaching injureth those who hear him, reckon me also among those who do this injury. For I cannot, in order to please you, see that one thing is best and chief of all, and say that another is.[5]

## CHAPTER XXIII.

#### CONSTANCY.

ABIDE in the precepts as in laws which it were impious to transgress. And whatsoever any man may say of thee, regard it not; for neither is this anything of thine own.

## CHAPTER XXIV.

#### HOW LONG?

1. How long wilt thou delay to hold thyself worthy of the best things, and to transgress in nothing the decrees of Reason? Thou hast received the maxims by which it behoves thee to live; and dost thou live by them? What teacher dost thou still look for to

whom to hand over the task of thy correction? Thou art no longer a boy, but already a man full grown. If, then, thou art neglectful and sluggish, and ever making resolve after resolve, and fixing one day after another on which thou wilt begin to attend to thyself, thou wilt forget that thou art making no advance, but wilt go on as one of the vulgar sort, both living and dying.

2. Now, at last, therefore hold thyself worthy to live as a man of full age and one who is pressing forward, and let everything that appeareth the best be to thee as an inviolable law. And if any toil or pleasure or reputation or the loss of it be laid upon thee, remember that now is the contest, here already are the Olympian games, and there is no deferring them any longer, and that in a single day and in a single trial ground is to be lost or gained.

3. It was thus that Socrates made himself what he he was, in all things that befell him having regard to no other thing than Reason. But thou, albeit thou be yet no Socrates, yet as one that would be Socrates, so it behoveth thee to live.

## CHAPTER XXV.

### PARTS OF PHILOSOPHY.

1. THE first and most necessary point in philosophy is the use of the precepts, for example, not to lie. The second is the proof of these, as, whence it comes

that it is wrong to lie. The third is that which giveth confirmation and coherence to the others, such as, Whence it comes that this is proof? for what is proof? what is consequence? what is contradiction? what is truth? what is falsehood?

2. Thus the third point is necessary through the second, and the second through the first. But the most necessary of all, and that when we should rest, is the first. But we do the contrary. For we linger on the third point, and spend all our zeal on that, while of the first we are utterly neglectful, and thus we are liars; but the explanation of how it is shown to be wrong to lie we have ever ready to hand.

## CHAPTER XXVI.

### MEMORABILIA.

Hold in readiness for every need, these—

"Lead me, O Zeus, and thou Destiny, whithersoever ye have appointed me to go, and may I follow fearlessly. But if in an evil mind I be unwilling, still must I follow."

"That man is wise among us, and hath understanding of things divine, who hath nobly agreed with Necessity."

But the third also—

"O Crito, if so it seem good to the Gods so let it be. Anytus and Meletus are able to kill me indeed, but to harm me, never."[1]

### THE END.

# NOTES.

### CLEANTHES' HYMN TO ZEUS.

1. Professor Mahaffy, in his *Greek Life and Thought*, quotes the full text of this noble Hymn, which, he thinks, "would alone redeem the Hellenistic age, as it stands before us, from the charge of mere artificiality and pedantry."

2. ἰῆς μίμημα λαχόντες μοῦνον. This is Zeller's reading, but not Professor Mahaffy's, who has ἑνὸς μίμημα.

## BOOK I.

### CHAPTER I.

1. "Enter by the door" (*cf.* S. John, x. 1). The parallelisms in thought and expression between Epictetus and the New Testament have often been noticed, and the reader will discover many others, to which I have not thought it necessary to draw attention.

2. "Conceit:" οἴησις, *Einbildung*.

3. "To be elated:" ἐπαίρεσθαι. One might translate, "to be puffed up," except that that expression is only used in a bad sense, and one may be "elated" in anything that is truly of the nature of the good. The Stoics distinguished between χαρά, joy, and ἡδονή, pleasure; not rejecting or despising the former.

## Chapter II.

1. τὰ μέν εἰσιν ἐφ' ἡμῖν, τὰ δὲ οὐκ ἐφ' ἡμῖν. A fundamental distinction in the Epictetean system, which he sometimes expresses by the phrases, τὰ ἡμέτερα and τὰ τῶν ἄλλων—things that are our own and things that belong to others ; or τὰ ἴδια and τὰ ἀλλότρια—things that are our proper concern, and things that are alien to us.

2. On the Mons Palatinus in Rome there stood a temple to Fever. Upton quotes from Gruter, p. xcvii., an interesting inscription to this divinity: Febri. Divæ. Febri. Sanctæ. Febri. Magnæ. Camilla. Amata. Pro. Filio. Male. Affecto. P.

## Chapter III.

1. There is excellent MS. authority for this reading of the passage, which, however, is not Schweighäuser's. The latter reads: "Be content with them, and pray to the Gods."

2. "Steward of the winds." A quotation from Homer, *Od.* x. 21.

## Chapter IV.

1. "Through not being dazzled," etc. Ἂν τὰς ὕλας μὴ θαυμάσῃ.

## Chapter VI.

1. Note that in this passage "God," and "the Gods" and "the Divine," are all synonymous terms.

2. Or "of names."

3. Some texts add "such as Good or Evil."

# NOTES.

### CHAPTER VII.

1. Apparently a proverb, which may be paralleled in its present application by Luther's "Pecca fortiter."

2. A complex or conjunctive proposition is one which contains several assertions so united as to form a single statement which will be false if any one of its parts is false—*e.g.*, "Brutus was the lover and destroyer both of Cæsar and of his country." The disjunctive is when alternative propositions are made, as "Pleasure is either good or bad, or neither good nor bad."

3. I have followed Lord Shaftesbury's explanation of this passage, which the other commentators have given up as corrupt. It seems clear that whether the passage can stand exactly in the form in which we have it, or not, Lord Shaftesbury's rendering represents what Epictetus originally conveyed.

4. According to the usual reading, a scornful exclamation—"*Thou* exhort them!" I have followed the reading recommended by Schw. in his notes, although he does not adopt it in his text.

### CHAPTER VIII.

1. The founder of the Cynic school was Antisthenes, who taught in the gymnasium named the Cynosarges, at Athens; whence the name of his school. Zeller takes this striking chapter to exhibit Epictetus's "philosophisches Ideal," the Cynic being the "wahrer Philosoph," or perfect Stoic. (Phil. d. Gr. iii. S. 752.) This view seems to me no more true than that the missionary or monk is to be considered the ideal Christian. Epictetus takes pains to make it clear that the Cynic is a Stoic with a special and separate vocation, which all Stoics are by no means called upon to take up. Like Thoreau, that modern Stoic, when he went to live at Walden, the

Cynic tries the extreme of abnegation in order to demonstrate practically that man has resources within himself which make him equal to any fate that circumstances can inflict.

2. τριβώνιον, a coarse garment especially affected by the Cynics, as also by the early Christian ascetics.

3. "Nor pity." Upton, in a note on *Diss.* i., 18. 3. (Schw.) refers to various passages in Epictetus where pity and envy are mentioned together as though they were related emotions, and aptly quotes Virgil (*Georg.* ii., 499):—

"Aut doluit miserans inopem, aut invidit habenti."

It will be clear to any careful reader that when Epictetus asserts that certain emotions or acts are unworthy of a man, he constantly means the "man" to be understood as his highest spiritual faculty, his deepest sense of reason, his soul. That we are not to pity or grieve means that that side of us which is related to the divine and eternal is not to be affected by emotions produced by calamities in mere outward and material things. St. Augustine corroborates this view in an interesting passage bearing on the Stoic doctrine of pity (*De Civ. Dei.* ix., 5; *Schw.* iv., 132):—

"Misericordiam Cicero non dubitavit appellare virtutem, quam Stoicos inter vitia numerare non pudet, qui tamen, ut docuit liber Epicteti nobilissimi Stoici ex decretis Zenonis et Chrysippi, qui hujus sectæ primas partes habuerunt, hujuscemodi passiones in animum Sapientis admittunt, quem vitiis omnibus liberam esse volunt. Unde fit consequens, ut hæc ipsa non putent vitia, quando Sapienti sic accidunt, ut contra virtutem mentis rationemque nihil possunt."

The particular utterances of Epictetus here alluded to by St. Augustine must have been contained in some of the lost books of the *Dissertations,* as nothing like them is to be found explicitly in those which survive, although the latter afford us abundant means for deducing the conclusion which St. Augustine confirms.

## NOTES. 197

4. This cake seems to form a ridiculous anti-climax. But it appears to have been a vexed question in antiquity whether an ascetic philosopher might indulge in this particular luxury (πλακοῦς). Upton quotes Lucian and Diogenes Laertius for instances of this question being propounded, and an affirmative answer given (in one instance by the Cynic, Diogenes). The youth in the text is being addressed as a novice who must not use the freedom of an adept.

5. Upton quotes from Cymbeline :—

"Hath Britain all the sun that shines ? Day, night,
Art they not, but in Britain ? Prythee, think,
There's living out of Britain !"

But Epictetus means more than this in his allusion to sun and stars. See Preface, xxiv. This passage would lead us to suppose that Epictetus believed in a personal existence continued for some time after death. In the end, however, even sun and stars shall vanish. See ii. 13, 4.

6. Being arrested by Philip's people, and asked if he were a spy, Diogenes replied, "Certainly I am, O Philip; a spy of thine ill-counsel and folly, who for no necessity canst set thy life and kingdom on the chances of an hour."

7. According to Upton's conjecture, these were gladiators famous for bodily strength; and also, one would suspect, for some remarkable calamity.

8. This highly crude view of the Trojan war might have been refuted out of the mouth of Epictetus himself. Evil-doers are not to be allowed their way because they are unable to hurt our souls, but the hurt may be in the cowardice or sloth that will not punish them.

9. By wearing his cloak half falling off, in negligent fashion. Nothing is finer or more characteristic in Epictetus than his angry scorn of the pseudo-Stoics of his day.

10 ἀνάκρινον τὸ δαιμόνιον. The allusion evidently is to the genius or divine spirit by which Socrates felt himself guided.

11. Crates was a disciple of Diogenes. His wife was named Hipparchia. Upton quotes Menander (*apud Diog. L.*), "Thou wilt walk about with me in a cloak as once did his wife with Crates the Cynic."

12. Danaüs, father of the fifty Danaidæ. Æolus is mentioned in *Od.* x. as having six sons and six daughters.

13. τραπεξῆας πυλαωρούς. *Il.*, xxi. 69.

14. That is, he capped the quotation by quoting the following line (*Il.*, ii. 24, 25). Not a very striking intellectual effort; but Epictetus evidently considered it a meritorious thing to know Homer well enough to quote him in one's sleep, and he was right.

15. From a poem of Cleanthes.


# BOOK II.

## CHAPTER I.

1. According to the view of James Harris, in a long and valuable note communicated to Upton, the "master-argument" was so called from the supreme importance of the issues with which it dealt. On these issues different leaders of the Stoics took different sides, Diodorus holding both future and past things to be *necessary*, Cleanthes both *contingent*, and Chrysippus past things to be necessary and future contingent. Any two of the three propositions mentioned in the text exclude the third. For modern philosophy the distinction between the possible and the certain in the phenomenal world has, of course, no real existence; the possible being simply that of which we do not know whether it will come to pass or not.

2. Of course Epictetus here speaks ironically : all this is just what it *is* the business of a thinker to do.

3. Epictetus, I suppose, means to complain that the current phrases of philosophy are dealt out in glib answer to great ethical questions, just as Homer might be quoted for an event in the life of Odysseus, by persons who in neither case think of gaining that vital conviction which only the strenuous exercise of one's own reason can produce. A little later he represents Hellanicus, the historian, as quoted on the distinction between good and evil, who never treated that subject. If it is to be a mere question of *authority*, one *name* is as good as another, since none is any use at all.

"Indifferent," be it observed, is *morally* indifferent—that which has *in itself* no bearing on our moral state. See Chap. II. 2.

4. The followers of Aristotle called themselves Peripatetics.

CHAPTER II.

1. The word in the Greek is περιστάσεις, literally *circumstances*, but the word is evidently used in a bad sense, as equivalent to afflictions. Doom is likewise etymologically a neutral word, but one which has received an evil meaning.

2. Socrates's faith in his genius or "Dæmon" was well known. In this passage from his *Apologia* (which Epictetus gives from a bad text), it is doubtless the manner only that conveyed the idea of mockery. Neither Socrates nor anyone else ever had better evidence of God's existence than His voice in our conscience.

CHAPTER IV.

1. Briefly, the three divisions seem to be Action, Character, and Judgment. The last is to be approached through training in logic, in the penetration of fallacies, etc., by which means a man is to

arrive at such an inward and vital conviction of the truth that he can never for a moment be taken off his guard by the delusion of Appearance.

2. Passions, passionless, τὰ πάθη, ἀπαθής.—See Index of Philosophic Terms.

## CHAPTER V.

1. *Euripides.*—Musonius Rufus, the teacher of Epictetus, is reported to have said, "Take the chance of dying nobly when thou canst, lest after a little death indeed come to thee, but a noble death no more."

2. This phrase of the "open door" occurs frequently in Epictetus, usually when, as here, he is telling the average nonphilosophic man that it is unmanly to complain of a life which he can at any time relinquish. The philosopher has no need of such exhortation, for he does not complain, and as for death, is content to wait God's time. But the Stoics taught that the arrival of this time might be indicated by some disaster or affliction which rendered a natural and wholesome life impossible. Self-destruction was in such cases permissible, and is recorded to have been adopted by several leaders of the Stoics, generally when old age had begun to render them a burden to their friends.

3. *Nay, thou shalt exist*, etc.—This is the sense given by Zeller's punctuation. Schweighäuser's text would be rendered, "Thou shalt not exist, but something else will," etc. Upton changes the text (on his own authority) by transposing an οὐκ. "Thou shalt exist, but as something else, whereof the universe has now no need."

4. This does not appear to have been the law in Epictetus's time, for he himself was educated while a slave. But it was a common provision in antique states.

5. The ceremony in manumitting a slave.

## CHAPTER VI.

1. Chap. VI. i. is a passage from the lost Fifth Book of the Discourses, preserved for us in a rather obscure Latin translation by Aulus Gellius. During a storm at sea, a certain Stoic on board was observed by him to look pale and anxious, though not indeed showing the signs of panic exhibited by the other passengers. Questioned afterwards by Gellius on this apparent feebleness in his professed faith, the Stoic produced the Fifth Book of Epictetus, and read this passage.

2. The third Earl of Shaftesbury, an enthusiastic student of Epictetus, had this dish of water and ray of light engraved, and placed, with the inscription, πάντα ὑπόληψις—All is Opinion—as an emblem at the front of his *Characteristics*. The passage, though interesting, is obscure. At one time the "appearances," φαντασίαι, are compared to the ray of light; at another, the doctrines (literally "arts," *i.e.*, arts of life taught by philosophy) and virtues. Probably the explanation is to be found in the view of the Stoics that at birth the human soul is a *tabula rasa*, or blank sheet; all our knowledge coming from without; that is, from the "appearances" which surround us. Moral and philosophic convictions are thus, like all other mental states, the result of external impressions.

## CHAPTER VII.

1. The school of Plato was continued at Athens under the title of the Academy. In its later days it produced little except logical puzzles.

2. "Friend, if indeed, escaping from this war, we were destined thereafter to an ageless and deathless life, then neither would I fight in the van nor set thee in the press of glorious battle. But now, since death in a thousand kinds stands everywhere against us, which no man shall fly from nor elude, we go; either we shall give glory to another, or he to us."—Sarpedon's speech, *Iliad* xii. 322-8.

3. General consent.—The well-known philosophic doctrine, that what all men unite in believing must be true, which has so often been made the basis of arguments against Scepticism in various forms.

## Chapter VIII.

1. See chap. IV. i.

2. He drew water by night for his gardens, and studied philosophy in the day.—*Diog. Laert.* [Upton.]

3. A most characteristic feature of the whole Stoic school was its treatment of ancient mythology and legend. These things were closely and earnestly studied, with a constant view to the deeper meanings that underlay the vesture of fable, an attitude which contrasts very favourably with Plato's banishment of the poets from his Republic for "teaching false notions about the Gods."

## Chapter IX.

1. Gyara, an island in the Ægean, used as a penal settlement.

## Chapter X.

1. *The captain . . . the driver*—literally, "to him who has knowledge" (of the given art).

2. Liberator—καρπιστής. The person appointed by law to carry out the ceremony of the manumission of slaves.

## Chapter XI.

1. This chapter seems to me to contain a truth expressed so baldly and crudely as to appear a falsehood. The reader's mind will be fixed upon the truth or falsehood according as he is or is not capable of reading Epictetus with understanding.

2. This earthen lamp was sold, according to Lucian, at the death of Epictetus for 3000 drachmæ (about £120).—*Adv. Indoct.* 13.

# NOTES. 203

### CHAPTER XIII.

1. Parodying a verse of Euripides on the stream of Dirce in Bœotia. The Marcian aqueduct brought water to Rome.

2. I adopt Upton's conjecture for the inexplicable 'ἐν βοὸς κοιλίᾳ.

### CHAPTER XVIII.

1. An eminent Cynic (also mentioned by Seneca and Tacitus).

### CHAPTER XXV.

1. This is the reading of one of the Christian Paraphrases. The other versions add the words πρὸς ἀλλήλους after ἐξ ὧν οὐ διαφερόμεθα, giving the sense "from things in which we do not differ from each other." It is no uncommon thing for all the versions of Epictetus to unite in a manifestly corrupt reading, and though in this case the received text is not an impossible one, I have thought myself justified in following the variant of the Paraphrase.

### CHAPTER XXVII.

1. There is an allusion to this curious feature of the Olympic contests in the Fourth Idyll of Theocritus. Casaubon (*Lect Theocr.* ad Idyll. 4) quoted by Schweighäuser, in his note on this passage (*Diss.* III. xv. 4), shows from Festus Pompeius that there was a statue in the Capitol of a youth bearing a spade after the manner of the Olympic combatants.

2. Euphrates, a Stoic philosopher, and contemporary of Epictetus. He was tutor of Pliny, the younger.

3. The pentathlos contended in five athletic exercises—viz., running, leaping, throwing the quoit, throwing the javelin, wrestling.

4. Much of this must refer to the period of probation or discipleship, for Epictetus is clear that the ordinary Stoic (who had not embraced the special mission of Cynicism) was not required to forsake his family, or his affairs, or his duties as a citizen, nor even justified in doing so.

## BOOK III.

### Chapter II.

1. The husk is, of course, the body. If it is maintained that Nature has made the ease of this our only proper pursuit, of course the altruistic, or social instincts, have to be rejected and denied.

2. The text is here almost certainly corrupt. It runs πῶς οὖν ὑπονοητικοί ἐσμεν, οἷς μὴ φυσική ἐστι πρὸς τὰ ἔκγονα φιλοστοργία. All the MSS. agree in ὑπονοητικοί, for which Schweighäuser desires to read προνοητικοί, and Wolf, ἔτι κοινωνικοί. Salmasius declares emphatically for πῶς οὖν ἐπινοεῖς ὅτι κοινωνικοί ἐσμεν, and this, with a slight alteration suggested to me by an eminent living scholar, is the reading I have adopted. Let us suppose that Epictetus said πῶς οὖν ὑπονοεῖς ὅτι κ.ε., and that this was written in the short lines common in Greek MSS. :—

ΠΩΣΟΥΝΥΠΟ<br>
ΝΟΕΙΣΟΤΙΚΟΙ<br>
ΝΩΝΙΚΟΙ

The second line, beginning with the same letter as the third, might easily be dropped by a transcriber, and the next transcriber would certainly change the resulting ὑπονωνικοί to ὑπονοητικοί. The existing reading might give the sense, "How are we, then, suspicious of those (if any there be) to whom Nature has given no affection for their offspring?"

3. Outward things—such as making provision for one's family, serving the State, etc.,—actions which are not directly concerned with our spiritual good.

# NOTES.

## CHAPTER III.

1. Phrygia, the birth-place of Epictetus, was one of the great centres of the wild and fearful cult of Cybele, whose priests gashed and mutilated themselves in the excitement of the orgie.

2. Philosophy is brought upon the scene, speaking first through the mouth of a Stoic, afterwards through that of an Epicurean, and the practical results of each system are exhibited.

3. The Athenians, rather than submit to Xerxes, abandoned their city to be plundered, and took to their fleet, the victory at Salamis rewarding their resolve.

Those who died at Thermopylæ were the three hundred Spartans under Leonidas, who held the pass against the Persian host till all were slain. Often as their heroism has been celebrated, perhaps nothing more worthy of their valour has been written than the truly laconic epitaph composed for them by Simonides:—

" Stranger, the Spartans bade us die :
Go, tell them, thou, that here we lie."

## CHAPTER IV.

1. The sense of human dignity was strong in Epictetus, and he would have it practically observed in men's relations with each other. Compare Ch. v. 7. Zeller must have overlooked these Fragments of Epictetus when he asserted (p. 301) that no Stoic philosopher had ever condemned slavery. So far as we know, however, this is the only condemnation of that institution ever uttered by any Pagan thinker. The usual Stoic view was laid down by Chrysippus, who defined the slave very much as Carlyle does, as a "perpetuus mercenarius"—a man "hired for life," from whom work was to be required, a just return for it being accorded (*operam exegendam, justa præbenda*). This utterance of Epictetus, as of one who knew slavery from within, and certainly was not inclined to exaggerate its discomforts, is noteworthy enough.

## Chapter V.

1. Administrator, διορθωτής; in Latin, *Corrector*—a State officer of whom inscriptions, etc., make frequent mention, but of whose functions not much appears to be known beyond what the present chapter of Epictetus reveals.

2. Cassiope was a port of Epirus, not far from Nicopolis, where Epictetus taught. Schw. conjectures that Maximus was sending his son to study philosophy at Nicopolis under Epictetus.

3. "For a correct view of these matters will reduce every movement of preference and avoidance to health of body and tranquillity of soul; for this is the perfection of a happy life."—Epicurus, *Diog. Laert.* x. 128. Epictetus's analysis of the Epicurean theory amounts to this, that the pleasure of the soul is the chief good, but that it is only felt through the body and its conditions.

4. *The overseer of youth.*—An officer in certain Greek cities. See Mahaffy's *Greek Life and Thought*, ch. xvii., on the organisation of the *ephebi*.

5. *Aid in works that are according to Nature.*—The Greek is—ἐν τοῖς κατὰ φύσιν ἔργοις παρακρατῇ. There is some difference of opinion among commentators as to the meaning of παρακρατῇ. Wolf translates, "hold the chief place" in natural works. Upton, Schw., and Long render it by "keep us constant," "sustain us," in such works. I do not see why we should not take the word in its plainest sense—that pleasure should *act together with other forces* in leading us to do well.

## Chapter VII.

1. *Zealous for evil things.*—Epictetus must mean things which they know to be evil—evil things *as* evil. It was a Socratic doctrine which we find again alluded to in this chapter, that no evil is ever willingly or wittingly done.

## NOTES.   207

2. A favourite theme of later Greek and of Roman comedy was the rivalship in love of a father and a son.

3. Admetus, husband of Alcestis, being told by an oracle that his wife must die if no one offered himself in her stead, thought to lay the obligation on his father, as being an old man with but few more years to live. The first verse quoted is from the *Alcestis* of Euripides; the second is not found in any extant version of that play.

4. Eteocles and Polyneices, sons of Œdipus, quarrelled with each other about the inheritance of their father's kingdom. Eteocles having gained possession of it, Polyneices brought up the famous seven kings, his allies, against Thebes, and fell in battle there by his brother's hand, whom he also killed. The verses quoted are from the *Phœnissœ* of Euripides.

5. Schweighäuser interprets this passage to mean that these men occupy the public places as wild beasts do the mountains, to prey on others. If we might read ὡς τὰ θηρία for ὡς τὰ ὄρη, we should get a less obscure sense, "haunt the wilderness—I should say the public places—like wild beasts." The passage is clearly corrupt somewhere.

6. Polyneices bribed Eriphyle with the gift of this necklace to persuade her unwilling husband to march with him against Thebes where he died.

### CHAPTER VIII.

1. The allusion is to *Odyssey*, v. 82-4. "But he was sitting on the beach and weeping, where he was wont; and tormented his spirit with tears and groanings and woes, and wept as he gazed over the barren sea."

2. *Let him pity.*—See Bk. I., ch. viii., *note* 3.

### CHAPTER IX.

1. *The conflagration.*—See Preface for an account of the Stoic Doctrine of the *Weltverbrennung*.

2. *Long* suggests that the words translated "air to air" might be equally well rendered "spirit to spirit" (ὅσον πνευματίου εἰς πνευμάτιον), thus finding a place for the soul in this enumeration of the elements of man. But this metaphysical division of man's nature into a spiritual part and a material part would have been wholly contrary to Stoic teaching, which admitted no existence that was not material. As a matter of fact, if any of the terms in this enumeration is to be understood as meaning soul or spirit, it will be fire rather than air.

3. Gods and Powers.—θεῶν καὶ Δαιμόνων.

## Chapter X.

1. *To strangle lions or embrace statues.*—Hercules did the former, and ostentatious philosophers sometimes did the latter in winter-time, by way of showing their power of endurance.

2. *The stamp of Nero.*—I believe there is no other record than this of any rejection of Nero's coins, and those which have come down to us are of perfectly good quality. He was declared a public enemy by the Senate, and possibly it was decreed at the same time that his coins should be withdrawn from circulation. Dion, quoted by Wise (*apud* Schweighäuser), reports that this was done in the case of Caligula, after the death of that tyrant.

3. *Lions at home, but in Ephesus foxes.*—"A proverb about the Spartans, who were defeated in Asia," notes the Scholiast on Aristoph. Pac., 1188-90.

## BOOK IV.

### Chapter II.

1. *Nor can I move without thy knowledge.*—From Homer, *Il.* x. 279, 280, Odysseus to Athene.

2. *The Genius of each man.*—τὸν ἑκάστου Δαίμονα.

## CHAPTER III.

1. *A way wherein to walk.*—Literally, the power of using a way. It seems to me likely that this term, way—ὁδός, here signifies the Stoic philosophy, just as in the early Church it was used to signify Christianity (*e.g.*, *Acts* xxii. 4, and xix. 9, 23).

## CHAPTER IV.

1. *Nor have any object in themselves.*—Readers of Lotze will be reminded of the term Fürsichseinheit, used by him to denote the self-centred quality of true Being. The Greek here is οὐκ αὐτὰ προηγούμενα, προηγούμενα, being the word used in Bk. I. viii. 13, and Bk. III. v. 5, for the leading objects or obligations of man.

2 *Would that I had you with me!*—In Long's translation the pronoun *you* is explained to mean God. I can see no reason for this interpretation. The words are, I think, supposed to be uttered by a disciple to his master: they are such as Epictetus may have heard from many of his own disciples as they left him to take their part in the world of action.

3. *Cautious assent*—*i.e.*, caution in allowing oneself to entertain the impressions of appearances.

## CHAPTER V.

1. The strong and growing yearning for some direct, personal revelation of God, some supernatural manifestation of His existence and care for men, is noted by Zeller as a special trait of Hellenistic times. Such a revelation must have been longed for by many as the only satisfying answer to the destructive logic of the Pyrrhonists, and men's minds were also of course led that way by the insistence of the Stoic thinkers upon the communion of the individual with God, as the most important of all possible relations. Hence the growth of many wild and orgiastic cults at this epoch—all based on the state of

ecstasy connected with their rites, which was ascribed to supernatural influence. With the Stoics this movement took the comparatively sober shape of attention to the established system of oracular divination. Zeller, however, shows that some Stoics were disposed to rationalise the revelations of the oracles by supposing a certain sympathy between the mind of the seer and the future events which led to the unconscious selection of means of divination which would exhibit the proper signs.—(Z. 339, 340.) Epictetus evidently thought more of God's revelation in the conscience than any other.

2. The story is told by Simplicius in his commentary on this chapter. Two friends, journeying together to inquire of the oracle at Delphi, were set upon by robbers; one of them resisted, and was murdered, the other either fled or made no effort on his companion's behalf. Arriving at the temple of Apollo, he was greeted with the following deliverance of the oracle:—

> "Thou saw'st thy friend all undefended die—
> Foul with that sin, from Phœbus' temple fly."

## BOOK V.

### CHAPTER I.

1. Simplicius explains that the oath was to be refused, because to call God to witness in any merely personal and earthly interest implies a want of reverence towards Him; but that if there were a question of pledging one's faith on behalf of friends, or parents, or country, it was not improper to add the confirmation of an oath.

2. Upton quotes allusions to these recitations from Juvenal, Martial, and Pliny. Authors would read their own works and invite crowds of flatterers to attend. Epict. *Diss.* iii., 23. (Schweighäuser), is a scornful diatribe against the pretentious people who held forth on these occasions, and the people who assembled to hear and applaud them. He contrasts with fashionable reciters and lecturers his own master, Rufus. "Rufus was wont to say, *I speak to no purpose, if ye have time*

# NOTES.

*to praise me.* And, verily, he spoke in such a way that every man who sat there thought that some one had accused him to Rufus, he so handled all that was going on, he so set before each man's eyes his faults."

3. Into vulgarity—εἰς ἰδιωτισμόν.

## CHAPTER II.

1. The sophism, or puzzle, called the Liar, ran thus :—A liar says he lies : if it is true, he is no liar ; and if he lies, he is speaking truth. The Quiescent (ὁ ἡσυχάζων) was an invention attributed by Cicero to Chrysippus (Acad. ii., 29). When asked of a gradually-increasing number of things to say when they ceased to be few and became many, he was wont to cease replying, or be "quiescent," shortly before the limit was reached—a device which we have some difficulty in regarding as a fair example of Chrysippus's contributions to the science of logic. For the master sophism see Bk. II. chap. i., *note* 1.

2. Plato, *Laws*, ix :—"When any of such opinions visit thee, go to the purifying sacrifices, go and pray in the temples of the protecting Gods, go to the society of men whom thou hast heard of as good ; and now hear from others, now say for thine own part, that it behoves every man to hold in regard the things that are honourable and righteous. But from the company of evil men, fly without a look behind. And if in doing these things thy disease give ground, well ; but if not, hold death the better choice, and depart from life."

3. *The true athlete.*—Literally, ascetic, ἀσκητής ; *i.e.*, practiser.

4. The Dioscuri, or Twins, Castor and Pollux, were the patron deities of sailors.

## CHAPTER VI.

1. *If viewed disjunctively.*—That is, if we say, It is day, or, It is night. This is a difficult chapter, and full of corruptions. The feast alluded to is, doubtless, the feast of life, where the Gods are the hosts.

## Chapter VII.

1. *Winter training.*—Such as the Roman troops underwent when in winter-quarters. They were accustomed to exercise themselves with arms of double the normal weight, and prepare themselves by marching, running, leaping, etc., for active service.

## Chapter XII.

1. The Pancratium was a contest in which boxing and wrestling were both allowable. For the Pentathlon, see Bk. II. chap. xvii., note 3.

## Chapter XVI.

1. This means, apparently, that the judgment has no right to do more than endorse the deliverances of the perceptive faculty. If a man commits any error, he does it under the conviction that it is in some way for his profit or satisfaction; that is, that there is something of the nature of the Good in it. He may be mistaken in this; but so long as he does not know where Good and Evil really lie, he can do no other than he does. The true course, then, for the philosopher is not to condemn him for his actions, but to show him the fundamental error from which they proceed. The expression, "assent," συγκατατίθεσθαι, is that used by Epictetus in II. vi., etc., where he speaks of the mind as being imposed on, or taken captive, by the outward shows of things.

## Chapter XX.

1. The Greek is 'Επειδὴ λόγος 'εστὶν ὁ διαρθρῶν καὶ ἐξεργαζόμενος τὰ λοιπά. διαρθρόω means, literally, to fashion with joints, hence constitute organically, with interdependence of parts. Long translates "analyse."

## NOTES.

2. *Modius.*—A measure of about two gallons.

3. Antisthenes, about 400 B.C., founder of the Cynic school, which was established by him in the gymnasium called the Cynosarges (hence the name). As a Cynic, his authority would, of course, be respected by the hearers of Epictetus. This investigation of terms, or names, is, indeed, the beginning of philosophy and the guide to truth in any sphere, but perhaps not every one is competent to undertake it. There must be a real and not merely a formal appreciation of the contents of each term. A primrose is one thing to Peter Bell and another to Wordsworth. The term, let us say, Duty, is one thing to a Herbert Spencer and another to a Kant.

### CHAPTER XXII.

1. "My friends, fly all culture," is an injunction reported of Epicurus.—(*Diog. L.* x. 6.) However, neglect of form in literary style was a characteristic of philosophic writers of the Hellenistic period, which was by no means confined to the Epicureans.

2. This passage is corrupt. I follow the reading adopted by Schweighäuser (after Wolf); but it may be noted that Schweighäuser's translation follows another reading than that which he adopts in his text, viz.—κινουμένου (being moved), instead of τεινομένου (being strained). The original, in all versions, is γινομένου, which makes no sense at all.—See *Preface*, xxiii.

3. The writings enumerated are, of course, works of Epicurus. When dying, he wrote in a letter to a friend (*Diog. L.* x. 22) that he was spending a happy day, and his last.

4. Stoic ἀπάθεια was anything but insensibility. Chrysippus held that many things in the Kosmos were created for their beauty alone.— *Zeller*, 171.

5. There is another short chapter on the arts of ratiocination and expression (I. viii. *Schw.*), which glances at the subject from a somewhat different point of view from that taken in the chapter which I have given. There Epictetus dwells chiefly on the danger that weak spirits should lose themselves in the fascination of these arts: "For, in general, in every faculty acquired by the uninstructed and feeble there is danger lest they be elated and puffed up through it. For how could one contrive to persuade a young man who excels in such things that he must not be an appendage to them, but make them an appendage to him?"

## CHAPTER XXVI.

1. The first of these quotations is from the Stoic Cleanthes, the second from a lost play of Euripides; in the third Epictetus has joined together two sayings of Socrates, one from the *Crito* and one from the *Apologia.* Anytus and Meletus were the principal accusers of Socrates in the trial which ended in his sentence to death.

# NOTES ON THE PRINCIPAL PHILOSOPHIC TERMS USED BY EPICTETUS.

[I give under this head only those terms the exact force of which may not be apparent to the reader in a mere translation.]

Αἰδήμων.—Pious, reverent, modest. The substantive is αἰδώς, the German Ehrfurcht (*Wilhelm Meister, Wanderjahre*, Bk. II. ch. ii.), a virtue in high regard with Epictetus, who generally mentions it in connection with that of "faithfulness," πίστις. In Wordsworth's poem, "My heart leaps up when I behold a rainbow in the sky," the "natural piety" which he prays may abide with him in his old age seems to be just that moral sensitiveness or αἰδώς which passes into reverence and worship in the presence of certain things, and into shame and dread in that of others.

Ἀπάθεια.—Peace—that is, peace from passions, πάθη. Πάθος was any affection of the mind causing joy or grief. As it appears from Bk. II. iii. 1., ἀπάθεια is not, in Epictetus, the state of absolute freedom from these passions, but that of being able to master them so that they shall not overwhelm the inner man.

Διαρθρωτικός.—That which *organises*, constitutes organically, forms into a system. From ἄρθρον, a joint. The word "analyse," by which Long translates διαρθροῦν, seems to me wanting in the formative sense expressed by the original.

Δόγμα.—An opinion, that which seems (δοκεῖν) true; generally in the special sense of a philosophic dogma.

Εὐροεῖν.—To prosper; literally, to flow freely. εὔροια, prosperity. A common Stoic phrase for a happy life.

Εὐσέβεια.—Religion, piety. σέβομαι—"*to feel awe* or *fear* before God and man, especially when about to do something disgraceful" *(Liddell and Scott);* to worship, respect, reverence.

Ἡγεμονικόν (τό).—The Ruling Faculty—that in a man which chooses, determines, takes cognizance of good and evil, and sways the inferior faculties (δυνάμεις powers) to its will. Lotze notes this *hegemonic* quality in the human soul as that which distinguishes it from the bundle of sensations into which the Association Philosophy would resolve it.

Θαυμάζειν.—To admire, be dazzled with admiration by, to worship, to be taken up with a thing so as to lose the power of cool judgment. A frequent word in Epictetus, the sense of which is precisely rendered in Hor. *Sat.* 1, 4, 28, "Hunc capit argenti splendor, stupet Albius aere."

Ἰδιώτης.—One of the vulgar, an unlettered person; in Epictetus, one uninstructed in philosophy. Originally the word meant one who remained in private life, not filling any public office, or taking part in State affairs. A man might be an ἰδιώτης, or "layman," with respect to any branch of science or art.

Καλὸς καὶ ἀγαθός.—The good and wise man—literally, beautiful and good. A standing phrase to denote the perfection of human character. καλὸς is a word sometimes difficult to render. Curtius connects it etymologically with Sanscrit, *kalyas*; Gothic, *hails*, =healthy.

Οἴησις.—"Conceit"—defined by Cicero as "Opinatio"—intellectual self-sufficiency, the supposing oneself to know something when one does not. "The first business of a philosopher," says Epictetus, "is to cast away οἴησις, for it is impossible that one can begin to learn the things that he thinks he knows" (*Diss.* II. xvii. 1). He is not, in short, to be "wise in his own conceit."

# NOTES.

ὄρεξις, ἔκκλισις, ὁρμή, ἀφορμή.—Pursuit, avoidance, desire, aversion. According to Simplicius (Comment. *Ench.* i.), ὄρεξις and ἔκκλισις were used by the Stoics to express the counterparts in outward action of the mental affections, ὁρμή and ἀφορμή, and were regarded as consequent upon the latter.

προαίρεσις.—The Will; but as used in Epictetus, this word implies much more than the mere faculty of volition. Literally, it means a choosing of one thing before another; in Epictetus, the power of deliberately resolving or purposing, the exercise of the reflective faculty being implied. It is hardly to be distinguished from τὸ ἡγεμονικόν, *q. v.*

προλήψεις.—" Natural Conceptions." See Preface, xxviii., xxix. The "primary truths" of Lord Herbert of Cherbury.

Συγκατατίθεσθαι.—To assent to or acquiesce in anything, to ratify by the judgment the emotions produced by external things or events, such as the sense of dread, or pleasure, or reprobation, which they arouse in us. To be on one's guard against the hasty yielding of this assent is one of Epictetus's main injunctions to the aspirant in philosophy.

Ταράσσεσθαι.—To be troubled; ἀ-ταραξία, tranquillity. Ταράσσειν is primarily to stir up, confuse, throw into disorder.

φαντασία.—An appearance; with the Stoics, any mental impression as received by the perceptive faculty before the Reason has pronounced upon it, a bare perception.

# INDEX OF REFERENCES.

[The references in the right-hand column are to the books, chapters, and verses of the *Dissertations*, to the chapters of the *Encheiridion*, and to the *Fragments*, in Schweighäuser's edition of Epictetus.]

## BOOK I.

Chap. I. 1 .................................*Frag.* III.
,, ,, 2-5 ...............................*Diss.* II. xi. 1-25.
Chap. II. ..................................*Diss.* I. xxii. 1-16.
Chap. III. .................................*Diss.* I. i. 1-17.
Chap. IV. 1 ..............................*Diss.* III. iii. 1-4.
,, ,, 2 ..................................*Diss.* I. xxix. 1-4 to λάβε.
,, ,, 3 ..................................*Diss.* I. xxv. 1-6.
Chap. V. ..................................*Ench.* I.
Chap. VI. .................................*Diss.* II. xiv.
Chap. VII. 1, 2 .........................*Ench.* II.
,, ,, 3 ..................................*Diss.* I. xv. 7, 8.
,, ,, 4-6 ..............................*Diss.* II. ix. 1-12.
,, ,, 7 ..................................*Frag.* LXXII.
,, ,, 8 ..................................*Diss.* III. xiii. 20-23.
Chap. VIII. ...............................*Diss.* III. xxii.

## BOOK II.

Chap. I. ....................................*Diss.* II. xix.
Chap. II. 1 ................................*Frag.* LXIX.
,, ,, 2, 3 ..............................*Diss.* II. v. 1-9.
,, ,, 4 ..................................*Diss.* II. xvi. 15.
,, ,, 5, 6 ..............................*Diss.* II. vi. 9-19.
,, ,, 7, 8 ..............................*Diss.* II. v. 10-20.

## INDEX OF REFERENCES.

Chap. III. 1, 2 .................... Ench. III., IV.
,, ,, 3 ........................... Diss. III. xix.
,, ,, 4, 5 ......................... Ench. V., VI.
Chap. IV. 1, 2 .................... Diss. III. ii. 1-10.
Chap. V. 1-3 ...................... Diss. II. i. 1-20.
,, ,, 4 ............................ Diss. III. xxiv. 94.
,, ,, 5 ............................ Diss. II. i. 21-29.
Chap. VI. 1 ....................... Frag. CLXXX.
,, ,, 2 ............................ Diss. III. iii. 20-22.
Chap. VII. 1-4 .................... Diss. I., xxvii.
Chap. VIII. 1 ..................... Diss. I. ix. 1-8.
,, , 2-6 .......................... Diss. III. xxvi. 1 36.
Chap. IX. 1 ....................... Diss. I. ix. 10-18.
,, ,, 2 ............................ Diss. I. xxv. 14-20.
,, ,, 3 ............................ Diss. I. xxix. 29.
Chap. X. 1-4 ...................... Diss. I. xix. 1-17.
,, ,, 5-6 .......................... Diss. IV. vii. 12-18.
,, ,, 7 ............................ Diss. I. xviii. 17.
,, ,, 8 ............................ Diss. IV. vii. 19-24.
Chap. XI. ......................... Diss. I. xviii. 1-16.
Chap. XII. ........................ Ench. VII.
Chap. XIII. 1, 2 .................. Ench. VIII.-IX.
,, ,, 3-6 .......................... Diss. II. xvi. 24-47.
Chap. XIV. ....................... Ench. X.
Chap. XV. ........................ Ench. XI.
Chap. XVI. ....................... Ench. XII.
Chap. XVII. ...................... Ench. XIII.
Chap. XVIII. 1, 2 ................ Ench. XIV.
,, ,, 3 ........................... Diss. I. xxv. 22-25.
,, ,, 4 ........................... Ench. XV.
Chap. XIX. ....................... Ench. XVI.
Chap. XX. 1 ...................... Ench. XVII.
,, ,, 2 ............................ Diss. IV. x. 9-17.
Chap. XXI. ....................... Ench. XVIII.-XXI.
Chap. XXII. ...................... Ench. XXII., XXIII.
Chap. XXIII. ..................... Ench. XXIV.
Chap. XXIV. ..................... Ench. XXV.
Chap. XXV. ...................... Ench. XXVI., XXVII.
Chap. XXVI. ..................... Ench. XXVIII.
Chap. XXVII. .................... Ench. XXIX.

## BOOK III.

Chap. I. .................................... *Ench.* XXX.
Chap. II. 1, 2 ........................... *Diss.* I. xxiii.
  ,,   ,, 3 7 ............................. *Diss.* II. v. 24-30.
Chap. III. 1-9 ........................... *Diss.* II. xx. 1-27.
Chap. IV. 1 ................................ *Diss.* I. xiii.
  ,,   ,, 2, 3 ........................... *Frag.* XLIII., XLIV.
Chap. V. .................................... *Diss.* III. vii.
Chap. VI. 1 ............................... *Frag.* LXXXII.
  ,,   ,, 2 ................................. *Frag.* XLV.
  ,,   ,, 3 ................................. *Frag.* LXVII.
Chap. VII ................................... *Diss.* II. xxii.
Chap. VIII. 1-10 ........................ *Diss.* III. xxiv. 1-49.
  ,,   ,  11 ............................ ,,   ,,   ,,  58-63.
  ,,   ,, 12 ............................ ,,   ,,   ,,  88-93.
Chap. IX. 1, 2 ........................... *Diss.* III. xiii. 1-17.
  ,,   ,, 3 .................................. *Frag.* CLXXVI.
  ,,   ,, 4 .................................. *Diss.* III. xiii. 18, 19.
Chap. X. 1 ................................. *Frag.* LXX.
  ,,   ,, 2 .................................. *Diss.* IV. v. 1-4.
  ,,   ,, 3-5 ................................ ,,   ,,   ,,  8-21.
  ,,   ,, 6 .................................. ,,   ,,   ,,  30-32.
  ,,   ,, 7 .................................. *Diss.* IV. v. $\begin{cases} 33 \text{ to } ἀγνώμονος. \\ 35\text{-}37. \end{cases}$

## BOOK IV.

Chap. I. .................................... *Ench.* XXXI.
Chap. II. 1, 2 ........................... *Diss.* I. xii. 1-7.
  ,,   ,, 3, 4 ............................. *Diss.* I. xiv. 1-17.
Chap. III. .................................. *Diss.* I. xvi.
Chap. IV. 1, 2 ........................... *Diss.* II. viii. 1-8.
  ,,   ,, 3 .................................. *Diss.* I. vi. 13 from ἄλλο—22.
  ,,   ,, 4-8 ................................ *Diss.* II. viii. 9-29.
Chap. V. .................................... *Ench.* XXXII.

## BOOK V.

Chap. I. 1-5 ............................. *Ench.* XXXIII. 1-6.
  ,,   ,, 6 .................................. *Diss.* III. xvi. 5-9.
  ,,   ,, 7-16 .............................. *Ench.* XXXIII. 7-16.

## INDEX OF REFERENCES.

Chap. II. 1-4..................Diss. II., xviii. 1-21 to ἀποθανόντων
,,   ,, 5, 6..................Diss. II. xviii. 23-32.
,,   ,, 7....................Diss. IV. xii. 19-21.
Chap. III. 1, 2 .:..............Diss. II. xii. 1-4.
,,   ,, 3, 4.................. ,,  ,,  ,, 17-25.
Chap. IV. ....................Ench. XXXIV.
Chap. V. .....................Ench. XXXV.
Chap. VI. ....................Ench. XXXVI.
Chap. VII. 1 .................Ench. XXXVII.
,,   ,, 2....................Diss. I. ii. 30-32.
Chap. VIII. ..................Ench. XXXVIII.
Chap. IX. ....................Ench. XXXIX.
Chap. X. .................... Ench. XL.
Chap. XI. ....................Ench. XLI.
Chap. XII. 1 .................Diss. III. i. 1-9.
,,   ,, 2....................Diss. ,, ,, 40-44.
,,   ,, 3, 4.................Diss. IV. xi. 22-29.
,,   ,, 5.................... ,,  ,,  ,, 35, 36.
Chap. XIII....................Ench. XLII.
Chap. XIV. ..................Ench. XLIII.
Chap. XV. ...................Ench. XLIV.
Chap. XVI. 1, 2 ..............Ench. XLV.
,,   ,, 3 ....................Diss. I. XXVIII. 1-9.
,,   ,, 4 .................... ,,  ,,  ,,  11-25.
Chap. XVII. .................Ench. XLVI.
Chap. XVIII. ................Ench. XLVII.
Chap. XIX. ..................Ench. XLVIII.
Chap. XX. 1 .................Diss. I. xvii. 1, 2.
,,   ,, 2-4................... ,,  ,,  ,, 4-12.
Chap. XXI. ..................Ench. XLIX.
Chap. XXII. 1, 2 ............. Diss. II. xxiii. 1-10.
,,   ,, 3-7.................. ,,  ,,  ,, 20-47.
Chap. XXIII. ................ Ench. L.
Chap. XXIV..................Ench. LI.
Chap. XXV. .................Ench. LII.
Chap. XXVI..................Ench. LIII.

---

*Printed by* WALTER SCOTT, *Felling, Newcastle-upon-Tyne.*

*Monthly Shilling Volumes. Cloth, cut or uncut edges.*

# THE CAMELOT SERIES.
EDITED BY ERNEST RHYS.   VOLUMES ALREADY ISSUED—

ROMANCE OF KING ARTHUR. Edited by E. Rhys.
THOREAU'S WALDEN. Edited by W. H. Dircks.
ENGLISH OPIUM-EATER. Edited by William Sharp.
LANDOR'S CONVERSATIONS. Edited by H. Ellis.
PLUTARCH'S LIVES. Edited by B. J. Snell, M.A.
RELIGIO MEDICI, &c. Edited by J. A. Symonds.
SHELLEY'S LETTERS. Edited by Ernest Rhys.
PROSE WRITINGS OF SWIFT. Edited by W. Lewin.
MY STUDY WINDOWS. Edited by R. Garnett, LL.D.
GREAT ENGLISH PAINTERS. Edited by W. Sharp.
LORD BYRON'S LETTERS. Edited by M. Blind.
ESSAYS BY LEIGH HUNT. Edited by A. Symons.
LONGFELLOW'S PROSE. Edited by W. Tirebuck.
GREAT MUSICAL COMPOSERS. Edited by E. Sharp.
MARCUS AURELIUS. Edited by Alice Zimmern.
SPECIMEN DAYS IN AMERICA. By Walt Whitman.
WHITE'S SELBORNE. Edited by Richard Jefferies.
DEFOE'S SINGLETON. Edited by H. Halliday Sparling.
MAZZINI'S ESSAYS. Edited by William Clarke.
PROSE WRITINGS OF HEINE. Edited by H. Ellis.
REYNOLDS' DISCOURSES. Edited by Helen Zimmern.
PAPERS OF STEELE & ADDISON. Edited by W. Lewin.
BURNS'S LETTERS. Edited by J. Logie Robertson, M.A.
VOLSUNGA SAGA. Edited by H. H. Sparling.
SARTOR RESARTUS. Edited by Ernest Rhys.
WRITINGS OF EMERSON. Edited by Percival Chubb.
SENECA'S MORALS. Edited by Walter Clode.
DEMOCRATIC VISTAS. By Walt Whitman.
LIFE OF LORD HERBERT. Edited by Will H. Dircks.
ENGLISH PROSE. Edited by Arthur Galton.
IBSEN'S PILLARS OF SOCIETY. Edited by H. Ellis.
FAIRY AND FOLK TALES. Edited by W. B. Yeats.
EPICTETUS. Edited by T. W. Rolleston.
THE ENGLISH POETS. By James Russell Lowell.
ESSAYS OF DR. JOHNSON. Edited by Stuart J. Reid.
ESSAYS OF WILLIAM HAZLITT. Edited by F. Carr.
LANDOR'S PENTAMERON, &c. Edited by H. Ellis.
POE'S TALES AND ESSAYS. Edited by Ernest Rhys.
VICAR OF WAKEFIELD. By Oliver Goldsmith.
POLITICAL ORATIONS. Edited by William Clarke.
CHESTERFIELD'S LETTERS. Selected by C. Sayle.
THOREAU'S WEEK. Edited by Will H. Dircks.
STORIES from CARLETON Edited by W. B. Yeats.
Autocrat of the Breakfast-Table. By O. W. Holmes.
JANE EYRE. By Charlotte Brontë.

London: WALTER SCOTT, 24 Warwick Lane, Paternoster Row.

# The Canterbury Poets.

EDITED BY WILLIAM SHARP.

In SHILLING Monthly Volumes, Square 8vo. Well printed on fine toned paper, with Red-line Border, and strongly bound in Cloth.

Cloth, Red Edges - 1s. | Red Roan, Gilt Edges 2s. 6d.
Cloth, Uncut Edges - 1s. | Pad. Morocco, Gilt Edges - 5s.

*THE FOLLOWING VOLUMES ARE NOW READY.*

KEBLE'S CHRISTIAN YEAR.
COLERIDGE. Ed. by J. Skipsey.
LONGFELLOW. Ed. by E. Hope.
CAMPBELL. Ed. by J. Hogben.
SHELLEY. Edited by J. Skipsey.
WORDSWORTH.
   Edited by A. J. Symington.
BLAKE. Ed. by Joseph Skipsey.
WHITTIER. Ed. by Eva Hope.
POE. Edited by Joseph Skipsey.
CHATTERTON.
   Edited by John Richmond.
BURNS. Poems ⎫ Edited by
BURNS. Songs ⎭ Joseph Skipsey.
MARLOWE. Ed. by P. E. Pinkerton.
KEATS. Edited by John Hogben.
HERBERT. Edited by E. Rhys.
HUGO. Trans. by Dean Carrington.
COWPER. Edited by Eva Hope.
SHAKESPEARE.
   Songs, Poems, and Sonnets.
   Edited by William Sharp.
EMERSON. Edited by W. Lewin.
SONNETS of this CENTURY.
   Edited by William Sharp.
WHITMAN. Edited by E. Rhys.
SCOTT. Marmion, etc.
SCOTT. Lady of the Lake, etc.
   Edited by William Sharp.
PRAED. Edited by Fred. Cooper.
HOGG. By his Daughter, Mrs Garden.
GOLDSMITH. Ed. by W. Tirebuck.
MACKAY'S LOVE LETTERS.
SPENSER. Edited by Hon. R. Noel.
CHILDREN OF THE POETS.
   Edited by Eric S. Robertson.
JONSON. Edited by J. A. Symonds.
BYRON (2 Vols.) Ed. by M. Blind.
THE SONNETS OF EUROPE.
   Edited by S. Waddington.
RAMSAY. Ed. by J. L. Robertson.
DOBELL. Edited by Mrs. Dobell.
DAYS OF THE YEAR.
   With Introduction by Wm. Sharp.
POPE. Edited by John Hogben.
HEINE. Edited by Mrs. Kroeker.

BEAUMONT & FLETCHER.
   Edited by J. S. Fletcher.
BOWLES, LAMB, &c.
   Edited by William Tirebuck.
EARLY ENGLISH POETRY.
   Edited by H. Macaulay Fitzgibbon.
SEA MUSIC. Edited by Mrs Sharp.
HERRICK. Edited by Ernest Rhys.
BALLADES AND RONDEAUS
   Edited by J. Gleeson White.
IRISH MINSTRELSY.
   Edited by H. Halliday Sparling.
MILTON'S PARADISE LOST.
   Edited by J. Bradshaw, M.A., LL.D.
JACOBITE BALLADS.
   Edited by G. S. Macquoid.
AUSTRALIAN BALLADS.
   Edited by D. B. W. Sladen, B.A.
MOORE. Edited by John Dorrian.
BORDER BALLADS.
   Edited by Graham R. Tomson.
SONG-TIDE. By P. B. Marston.
ODES OF HORACE.
   Translations by Sir S. de Vere, Bt.
OSSIAN. Edited by G. E. Todd.
ELFIN MUSIC. Ed. by A. Waite.
SOUTHEY. Ed. by S. R. Thompson.
CHAUCER. Edited by F. N. Paton.
POEMS OF WILD LIFE.
   Edited by Chas. G. D. Roberts, M.A.
PARADISE REGAINED.
   Edited by J. Bradshaw, M.A., LL.D
CRABBE. Edited by E. Lamplough.
DORA GREENWELL.
   Edited by William Dorling.
FAUST. Edited by E. Craigmyle.
AMERICAN SONNETS.
   Edited by William Sharp.
LANDOR'S POEMS.
   Selected and Edited by E. Radford.
GREEK ANTHOLOGY.
   Edited by Graham R. Tomson.
HUNT AND HOOD.
   Edited by J. Harwood Panting.

London: WALTER SCOTT, 24 Warwick Lane, Paternoster Row.